The Divine Comedy
As Told for Young People
by Joseph Tusiani

Library of Congress Cataloging-in-Publication Data

Tusiani, Joseph 1924-
   Dante's Divine Comedy / as told for young people by Joseph Tusiani.
   p.cm.
   Summary: A prose retelling of Dante's poem about a journey through Hell, Purgatory and Paradise.
   ISBN 1-881901-29-7
   1.Dante Alighieri, 1265-321—Adaptations-Juvenile literature. [1. Dante Alighieri, 1265-1321—Adaptations.] I. Dante Alighieri, 1265-1321. Divina Commedia. II. Title.
   PS3539.U88 D36 2001
   813'.54—<:d21

                                  2001038835

Printed and Bound in Canada

On the cover Domenico di Michelino's painting of Dante illustrating his work, in Santa Maria del Fiore, Florence. Illustrations are by Gustave Dorè.

For information and for orders,write to **Legas**:

P.O. Box 149
Mineola, New York
11501, USA

3 Wood Aster Bay
Ottawa, Ontario
K2R 1D3 Canada

Legaspublishing.com

Dante's *Divine Comedy*

As Told for Young People

by Joseph Tusiani

LEGAS

Hell

The Dark Forest.

To Pamela A. Tusiani

In memoriam

TABLE OF CONTENTS

Inferno

Purgatory

Paradise

CHAPTER ONE
THE DARK FOREST

How would you feel if, awakening in the deep of night, you found yourself no more in your room but in a thick, dark forest called the Wilderness of Death? You would wonder how you got there, and would only remember that it was still daylight, and you were walking home on a comfortable road you knew quite well when suddenly you began to feel sleepy, very sleepy, until you could hardly see the road before you and hardly remember that you had a home to go to.

But there you are, in the thick, dark Forest of Death, and now your name is Dante, and Dante means something new and old – it means Mankind, for you are now all men in one. If you leave the forest alive, the whole world will be saved; if you do not, everybody will die with you. But will you ever be able to get out of this wilderness? Perhaps the morning light will tell you which path to take; but will the sun rise again?

The sun rises at last after a night of bewilderment and sorrow. Only at this moment can Dante feel hopeful again. Not far from the end of the Forest of Death he sees a hill already bright with the rays of the sun. Now everything is clear in his mind: that hill is the height of joy and freedom, and that sun is the light that saves every human soul from Darkness Everlasting. Still panting and with all his thoughts still running away from the horror of the forest, Dante starts walking toward the hill; but at the very beginning of it something he sees tells him that he will never be able to climb it. First, a spotted, nimble LEOPARD, then a horrible, hungry LION, and now a lean, murderous SHE-WOLF is blocking his way. Dante finds himself between two deaths: if he turns back to the forest he will die in its depth; and if he tries to climb the hill he will be slain by the ravenous She-Wolf. How long does he remain in front of the three wild animals? He does not know. He only knows that the three beasts in some strange way resemble something he knows very well– his own past. The Leopard looks like his own lust; the Lion, like his own pride; the She-Wolf, like his own greed.

As he is turning slowly back into the forest, Dante seems to remember that he himself is responsible for the presence of the three wild beasts at the foot of the hill, for at this moment it is not they that fight Dante, but it is Dante fighting Dante, his past wickedness rising against his present desire for life.

Dante has lost all hope when suddenly a shadow appears to him–VIRGIL, the poet of the *Aeneid*. Think how you would feel if Shakespeare appeared to you in your worst predicament, and you will understand Dante's feelings in the presence of the greatest poet of ancient Rome. But there is a difference. Virgil had lived and died before the birth of Christ, which means that at this moment Dante, a Christian, is found in the Forest of Sin not by another Christian but by a pagan who would have given the world for the opportunity of living in the Christian era.

"Help me! Save me from that beast which makes my soul and body tremble!" cries Dante after assuring Virgil of his great love and long study of his work. Virgil replies that he will help Dante provided that he follow him. But where does he want to take him? He will take him through the eternal darkness of the Lost Souls not only to make him see where one goes who through one's own fault slips into the Forest of Sin but also to prove to him that, even from the viewpoint of sheer human reason, it does not pay to abandon the road that leads to freedom and salvation.

When Dante hears that at the end of his unusual but necessary journey he will be able to see the Gate of Paradise, he tells Virgil that he is willing to do anything, to face anything, even the dangers and devils of Hell, so great is his desire to reach home and find peace and joy again. But then, as he is following Virgil, who really meant what he said, Dante is overcome with sudden fear. Who wouldn't be? There you are, right behind a man you respect very highly, a great man who cannot lie and yet, being human, might also be wrong. You have been told you must hear the cries and laments of the souls forever lost in Hell; which means you must go there with your body, not with your imagination alone. But what if you should never get out of such a place? You would die anyway. Why, then, this trip? If you are bound to die tomorrow a more fierce and cruel death, why not die now in this dark forest?

At this point Virgil, who is more or less Dante's own reason, tells a beautiful story of heavenly mercy and love. "I was in Limbo," he says, "when a lady came to me, so blessed and radiant, I asked her at once what I could do for her. Her eyes were shining like all stars made one when with a whisper of heaven she said to me: 'A man who is my friend, but not a friend of Fortune, is so impeded on the barren shore that I'm afraid I have come here too late. Oh, fly to him, and with your learned words and whatever you think necessary for his salvation, help him so that once more I may rejoice. I, who am asking you to go, am Beatrice. Love made me come, and bids my lips to speak.'" Virgil tells Dante how Beatrice then told him it had been the Blessed Virgin herself who had first seen his danger and felt sorry for him. But Dante seems to remember one thing – the name of Beatrice and her words, "A man who is my friend, but not a friend of Fortune." Does she love him so much even from Heaven? Hasn't she forgotten him despite his many sins and his enmity with her God? Virgil speaks on, but Dante can only think of that name and those words. He

12

realizes that, being in Heaven, she knows quite well that it was he who wanted to stray from home and fall into the Wilderness of Death; and yet she did not want Virgil to know that he did not deserve help.

Ten long, sad years have passed since the day of her death, and yet she is more alive than ever, more beautiful and charitable than ever. For the first time Dante understands what true love is, and knows, thanks to the Blessed Lady and Beatrice, there is still hope for his salvation. "O merciful Beatrice, who came to my rescue!" he cries at last, his mind whirling with thoughts of remorse and gratitude, his heart overflowing with remembrances of the past. And, turning to Virgil, "Let us go," he says, "for what you want I now want too. You are my teacher and my lord and guide."

As little flowers, closed and bent by the frost of the night, open their petals on their stems again as soon as the morning sun restores them with its warmth, so does the name of Beatrice renew Dante's courage now that the road turns suddenly bitter and steep.

CHAPTER TWO
THE BOAT OF CHARON

I am the entrance to the painful city,
I am the entrance to eternal grief,
I am the entrance to a lost people.

Justice compelled my maker high above,
And so I was created by divine
Omnipotence, deep wisdom, and first love.

Only eternal beings lived before
1 was created , and I last forever:
Leave hope behind you, passing through this door.

These words are carved in black above the Gate of Hell. Though you wonder for a moment how it was possible for God's Love to create this eternal place of suffering, you are terrified by the meaning of the last line, "Leave hope behind you, passing through this door." It takes no intelligence to understand that those who enter here will never come out. That is why Dante, his mind a sudden storm of fear and horror, turns to his guide and says: "Master, those words frighten me." But by replying, "You must not fear but simply trust me now," Virgil seems to reassure him; and since words alone are powerless in difficult moments, he takes Dante by the hand and smiles at him.

The gate is now behind them, and it is too late to think of going back. If you have seen the sand tossed by an angry wind into a blinding whirl, you have a faint notion of what it is that strikes your ears at this moment— a din of wails and shrieks and sobs and cries in all languages and dialects. The air you breathe is black, and black is the sky overhead — if you can call it sky; yet you see shadows and shadows running in all this blackness. These are the souls of the OPPORTUNISTS, mixed with those angels who at the dawn of creation were neither for God nor Lucifer but for themselves. Dante would like to know more about them; but what is there to know about people who on earth were neither alive nor dead? They were neither Republican nor Democrat, neither Guelph nor Ghibelline, neither your friends nor your enemies, but this or that according to the moment or the wind. They never had an idea of their own, either good or bad, and contributed nothing to society; they were, rather, a menace to their own country in as much as by their very lack of participation in public affairs they either increased the number of its foes or diminished that of its defenders. But look at them now, running behind a flag, any flag, and

*Charon and the
River Acheron.*

stung and stimulated by wasps and hornets which make their faces stream with blood, sucked at their feet by loathsome worms.

Dante knows that he is not in Hell yet, for he sees an innumerable throng of people waiting on the shore of the ACHERON, the river which they must cross to be in the presence of MINOS, the barking demon with the judging tail. Why are they so eager to reach the place of their timeless torture? Governed by the instinct of self-preservation, no man on earth is ever anxious to go to the place of his own execution. Why, then, are these souls so impatiently waiting to be ferried over to the other side of the Acheron? We shall know when we get to the river.

"You damned creatures! You damned creaures!" These words suddenly resound with an echo that lingers over the sinister tide of the stream. Everybody has been waiting for this moment, yet everybody seems to freeze with fright. Virgil and Dante, too, look toward the river. They seee nothing at first; then something strangely "white and red" pierces the darkness like the point of a flaming sword, and it grows nearer and nearer, larger and larger. A boat is finally seen near the shore with an old old man in it —CHARON. But only two things can one see of him—his beard and his eyes. His beard is ancient white, which means that you must think of two wide and bushy forests withering, as it were, on his cheeks. His eyes are two enormous wheels of fire endlessly rotating, and their flames are so fierce as to seem on the verge of destroying beard and hair in one huge conflagration. Turning to the waiting throng , and with an understatement full of infernal irony, CHARON shouts: "Do not ever hope to see heaven!" which perhaps means, "Say good bye to your God, all of you." But the name of God is too sacred and no soul in Hell will ever dare mention it.

Dante does not know if CHARON has already singled him out in the crowd. When he hears these other words, "I'm here to take you to the other shore, into eternal darkness, fire and ice," he is bewildered, and would like to tell the old demon-captain that he is not one of them, being still alive. Why doesn't Virgil speak out for him? But it is not hard for Charon to notice a living body among dead souls — something that has never happened before in all his centuries of service. Enraged, he shouts: "Hey, you over there, go away from these dead people, you living soul!" Dante is too frightened to say a word or even budge. Seeing that he does not move, Charon says with an angrier voice: "Not here! A lighter boat than mine will give you passage." Dante does not understand the meaning of these words. If he did, he would rejoice at being refused passage on Charon's boat which can only take passengers for whom there is no longer any hope of salvation. But Virgil comes to his rescue: "Charon, let not your anger kill you. This is willed there, where what is willed is done: so speak no more." Let us remember this phrase, "This is willed there, where what is willed is done." It is our password through Hell, and its means "It is God's Will."

As if struck by the sudden blow of a whip, Charon mumbles incoherent sounds until his woolly cheeks are utterly still. But the effect of those words on the souls on the shore is quite different. A storm of protest breaks out among them. They begin to curse God, their parents, grandparents, great grandparents, the place and the day of their birth, wishing not to have been born. It is a horrible sight: their faces have suddenly turned pale and, becoming visible for the first time, look like one immense lightning in a dark sky; the gnashing of their teeth can be heard like a thunder echoing from shore to shore. There is no rain save that of their tears, which, falling on the ground, seems to soak the entire earth.

It is now time to leave. Beckoning not with his hand but with the glowing coal of his eyes, Charon bids all the souls on board, and those who are not quick to obey the signal of his glance are mercilessly smitten by the one weapon in his hands — the oar. Who can tell the number of the souls that are now crowding the boat of Charon? To Dante it seems impossible that so many people have died on earth; and he does not yet know that, before the vessel will have reached the other shore, another throng will be awaiting the return of Charon. Dante can only compare them to the yellow, dead leaves falling one after the other in autumn, for, as the branch of a tree is withered and barren when all its leaves have fallen, so is the shore now that the souls are going out upon the darkened waves.

"My son," says Virgil, "all those who die in mortal sin come here from every land; and they are eager to cross the river because God's justice pricks them so, that fear becomes desire." In other words, a soul that has lost God sees and feels God's justice like a threatening sword hanging overhead, and such is its fear of it that it can think of nothing better than running away from it and hiding in its own eternal darkness. But— who knows — at this moment Dante remembers one thing —Virgil's words, "My son!" For the first time Virgil has called him "son." He is still savoring the joy of this word when a thunderbolt and then a red light overcome his senses.

Minos, the Judge of Hell.

CHAPTER THREE
THE ENDLESS STORM

When he awakens, Dante finds himself on the brink of a valley, called the Valley of the Abyss. It is deep and dark and cloudy. A thick, black mist is over it, and gives him a painful sensation of blindness. The only thing he can see is the pallor on Virgil's face. But Virgil is not afraid of the blind world into which he and Dante are now descending. It is pity for the people they are about to see which makes him look pale and sad. For the first time Dante is made to notice the difference between sin and sinner. Throughout our journey, therefore, we too must never make the mistake of confusing man with man's sin. Man as such is still worthy of our compassion because we are made of the same flesh and blood, and can commit the same sins; but man's sin as such must always be despised because it is the thing that soils God's image in us. Cancer is a horrible thing, yet the remembrance of one who has died from cancer is still very dear to us.

Dante and Virgil are now in the FIRST CIRCLE of Hell, called LIMBO. The souls in this place are neither happy nor unhappy, neither punished nor rewarded. The First Circle of Hell is not really Hell then, inasmuch as there is no suffering. When they were on earth, these people lived a good life; only they did not know God and died without baptism. In the middle of this Circle there is a castle, a beautiful castle all lit up, protected by seven rows of walls and surrounded by a lovely stream and an ever green lawn. In this castle live the greatest poets of ancient Greece and Rome, and on the nearby lawn sit the greatest philosophers talking of beautiful things.

Among these people, and especially in the presence of Homer, Dante feels very important and almost forgets that his trip has hardly begun. But suddenly the light disappears, the green lawn fades out of sight, and the barking of a dog pierces the air with a sinister sound. Dante realizes that he is now in a new place, lower and narrower— the SECOND CIRCLE of Hell.

Look there at the entrance. There is a man sitting and barking like a dog. Who is he? What is he doing there? And who are those people who come in front of him, stay less than a second, and are then plunged down like stones into a deep well? The barking man is MINOS, the one who decides to which circle of Hell a soul must go. But don't think for a moment that there is any sense of democracy in the way this trial is conducted. This judge does not have to see whether a soul is guilty or innocent. Those who come near his bench are all guilty. God has already judged them. Minos' task is to send them at once to the place where they belong — thieves with thieves, murderers with murderers, traitors with traitors, and so forth. When a soul comes before His Honor, I mean before His Horror, he sees in a flash what sin it has committed and died with, and if that particular soul must go to the seventh circle he wraps his tail around himself seven times. For Minos' coiling tail is at least twenty-five times as long as his body.

Waiting for his turn to come before Minos, Dante recalls the last line carved on the Gate of Hell, "Leave hope behind you, passing through this door!" Perhaps reading Dante's thoughts, the barking judge interrupts his work for a while, and shouts: "Let not the wideness of the gate deceive you; and think twice before you enter!" But Minos does not know that it is God Himself Who allows this living man to travel through the world of death, and so Virgil uses once more the password that should overcome every obstacle: "This is willed there, where what is willed is done." At these words Minos' enormous body blocks the entrance no more, and Virgil and Dante enter the den of the Endless Storm where the sin of lust is punished forever.

Dante finds himself in the midst of a tornado— a tornado— compared to which all the hurricanes on earth are a pleasant, cool breeze. Here the winds are not blowing seventy or eighty miles an hour because not time but only eternity exists in Hell; and they make Dante think of a stormy sea because a stormy sea is the only thing he still can think of. Imagine what would happen to a flock of little birds caught in a tornado. They would be tossed up and down, down and up, and, overwhelming the balance of their wings, the wind would thrust them now against a pole, now against the trunk of a tree, without mercy, without rest. At the end of the tornado there would certainly be not one little bird alive. Something like this happens in the Second Circle, with the difference that the souls caught in the Endless Storm know that the ruinous wind will never cease.

Dante recognizes CLEOPATRA among these new sinners. Turning then to his guide, "O Poet," he says, "I would so much like to talk to those two who even in the storm are so close to each other. "When the wind bends them toward us, beg them in the name of Love, and they will come," replies Virgil.

The gusty wind is roaring and deep darkness hovers all about. It is not easy to see when the two lovers, swept by the storm in its circular fury, will be passing again overhead. But this is the time. "O poor, poor souls," Dante cries out, "come and speak to us, if you are allowed to do so." How is it that Dante has not begged them in the name of Love? But he has. For the first time a voice of compassion has been heard in Hell. Only a person who knows what love is can understand, if not forgive, two souls condemned to be forever together so that each may forever remind the other not of the past moment of pleasure but of the eternity of pain ahead. But who are they? What have they done to deserve eternal punishment?

19

As soon as they hear that strange voice of pity, the two souls come down as two doves would fly back to their nest. How good it would be for them to find rest in man's compassion now that they know that God will never forgive them! When Dante learns that they are FRANCESCA DA RIMINI and PAOLO MALATESTA, his mind is suddenly overcome with the remembrance of the sad story of their death. He was twenty years old when the news of that tragedy reached Florence. He even remembers that everybody felt sorry for them, and no one had thought that God in His infinite mercy would not forgive them.

Francesca was very beautiful but still very young when her father, Guido Vecchio da Polenta, gave her in marriage, for political reasons, to Gianciotto Malatesta, the deformed Lord of Rimini. This was rather common in those days; but what was uncommon and cruel, in the case of Francesca's marriage, was how it was performed. Perhaps because he was too busy, or perhaps because he thought that his ugliness and deformity would frighten his young, innocent bride, Gianciotto decided to send his own brother Paolo, a very handsome youth, to represent him at the wedding ceremony. Little did Paolo know that that was the beginning of a relationship destined to end in blood. Did Francesca believe that Paolo was Gianciotto? Or was she told, when she reached the Malatesta castle in Rimini, that Paolo was only her brother-in-law? During the ten years that followed, Francesca was torn between her secret love for Paolo and her devotion to her husband. Paolo seemed to embody everything beautiful and good; Gianciotto, on the other hand, reminded her of war and bloodshed, for, though lame and deformed, he was a brave and ruthless soldier. Thus Francesca lived between dream and reality, her heart and mind in constant battle, until one day...

It is Francesca speaking now:

"We were, one day, reading of Lancelot—
how Love took hold of him—for sheer delight:
alone we were but with no evil thought.

"Several times that very reading took
our glances off the page, and made us pale,
till we were won by something in the book.

"When to the point we came where that great lover
 kissed on a mouth the fondness of a smile,
this man, who will be here with me forever,

"sealed on my lips the passion of his kiss ...

20

At Francesca's side, Paolo is weeping, and Dante is moved to pity by those tears. Perhaps he would like to know if the two were killed by Gianciotto on the day of that reading, or if that kiss was only the beginning of their sinful love. He knows that, in spite of every extenuating circumstance, not a man but God himself has been offended. His mind sees very clearly that these "poor souls" are guilty and do not deserve his compassion; his heart, on the other hand, feels extremely sorry for them. And so he does not know what to do or what to say. If he expresses his compassion and takes sides with Francesca and Paolo, he goes against God who has judged them; yet he, too, is human and weak, and cannot bear the thought that a moment, or even a year, or even a lifetime of wrong pleasure, should lead to an eternity of torture. Now he begins to understand why Virgil wants to take him through all the Circles of Hell—to show him that rebellion to the laws of God can lead but to disaster.

The Endless Storm resumes its fury, and, cursing the man who took their lives, the two souls are sucked up by the wind again, nevermore to hear a sound of pity. And this is only the least of all the punishments in Hell. What will be next? And will Dante meet people who once were dear to him? Thinking again of the two lovers' fate, his mind overwhelmed by what he has seen and heard, he faints and falls as a dead body falls.

Paolo and Francesca.

21

CHAPTER FOUR
DARK RAIN AND ROLLING ROCKS

When he comes to, Dante sees new tormented souls and hears new laments. With Virgil he is now in the THIRD CIRCLE where the GLUTTONS are punished. They are those who on earth believe only in one god — their stomach. They are those who do not eat to live but live to eat; people, in other words, who for the pleasure of food and drink forget honor, duty, dignity, family, fatherland, and everything. When such people die, in this place they continue their meal which consists of stinking mud. In fact, the Third Circle is a gray, livid marsh in which all these souls are immersed. A black rain mixed with hail and snow falls upon them, and so horrible is the stench of the earth that receives it that Dante is aware of it long before he sees a huge three-headed monster furiously barking over the pond. This monster is CERBERUS.

Cerberus has indeed three heads, one of which looks human with its black and greasy beard. His eyes are flaming-red, his belly is wide, and his hands are sharply clawed. This strange wild beast barks like a dog, and his barking, coming out of three throats, fills, as it were, the Third Circle with three thunderbolts in one. Squatting near the entrance, Cerberus bends over the water of the marsh and, clutching now one soul and now another, skins and tears it to countless pieces. Deep in the mud, the wretched ghosts turn now on their right and now on their left, they too barking like dogs.

When Cerberus sees Virgil and Dante standing near the entrance to the cave, he opens his three mouths and shows his fangs. Dante is sure that, as he did before in the presence of Charon and Minos, Virgil will pronounce even now the magic password, "It is willed there, where what is willed is done." But to his amazement, Virgil does not say a word. He simply bends to the ground, takes up two fistfuls of dirt and flings it into the beast's gaping throats. Dante at first does not understand, but, when he sees Cerberus fully intent on devouring that dirt like a dog quieted by a bone, he realizes that in this Circle the one thing these souls listen to is the sound of their own hungry jaws.

Among these souls Dante meets CIACCO, a Florentine friend, who tells him that, in less than three years, Florence will be the scene of a bloody civil war, since Pride, Envy, and Greed have set all hearts on fire. Dante does not seem to pay much attention to Ciacco's knowledge of the future, so great is at this moment his desire to know where some of his other friends are. "They are down among the blacker souls," replies Ciacco, "and if you go that far, you'll meet them all."

Passing through that filthy mixture of rain, mud, and snow, and trampling on the souls half-buried in it, Virgil and Dante reach the end of the cave, and are now at the door of the FOURTH CIRCLE where Plutus, the great enemy, is waiting.

PLUTUS, the ancient god of wealth, is the one who watches the entrance to the Fourth Circle where the MISERS and the SQUANDERERS are punished, those who on earth devote all their thoughts and energies to accumulating money, and those who, on the contrary, destroy their own and other people's riches without ever thinking of the good that they could do with what they squander. When you enter this Circle, the fourth step down into the Underworld, you understand at once certain things which were vague and foggy in your mind until this very moment. These new sinners remind you, by contrast, of millions and millions of people who starve, of children dying of malnutrition, of old beggars trembling from the cold, and so you realize that those who are responsible for so much poverty and sorrow cannot but pay for it. This is indeed the place of Justice.

"Pape Satan, Pape Satan aleppe," shouts Plutus, turning angrily to Virgil and Dante. What does he mean by these words? He probably means, "His Majesty the Devil has long been waiting." But Virgil knows what to do. He simply says, "It is willed there..." and at these words Plutus falls limp as the swollen sail of a boat if the mast suddenly breaks. Thus Dante and Virgil can step down into the new frightening cave.

A loud thundering noise strikes Dante's ears. He thinks of two huge waves of the sea crashing against each other. What is it? Despite the full darkness (it must be midnight now on earth), he sees an enormous quantity of huge rocks rolling. At first they seem to be moving by themselves, but then Dante notices that each rock is rolled by a man not with his hands but with his chest. Pushing the dead weights, the Misers and the Squanderers come from the opposite direction and, in the middle of the Circle, clash against one another, howling in despair; then each man turns round his rock and begins to roll it backward till all meet and clash once more at the extremity of the Circle.

And to think that all these people were considered lucky on earth! Virgil tells Dante about Dame Fortune, and Dante, struck by the sight and the nature of this new torture, listens to his guide with great attention. What men on earth call luck is no luck at all, for, if not used well and for the right purpose, money and wealth become a crushing weight.

"We are not allowed to stay here long," says Virgil to Dante, and so they both hasten across the Circle to the brink of the next descent. There they see a narrow stream of black water; they follow it, and come to a marsh called Styx. In the MARSH OF STYX, which is the FIFTH CIRCLE of Hell, are punished the ANGRY and the GLOOMY, those who, forgetting every sense of sweetness and charity, with the explosion of their anger make of this earth a place of terror, and those who with their ever gloomy disposition make life miserable to themselves and those around them. The Marsh of Styx takes, so to speak, good care of them. The souls of the Angry are plunged naked into the muddy water, and keep doing what they used to do when alive — they strike and slap one another not only with their hands but also with their heads, their chests, and their feet. The souls of the Gloomy, too, do even here what they used to do on earth. Deep in the mud, they sigh and sob, and with their laments make the water bubble at the surface.

But at this point Dante's eyes are struck by something quite unusual and utterly unexpected. "Master, there, up there, look! It is a tower. And those two lights, what are they? And what's the meaning of that other fire giving signals?" Dante is frantic, and Virgil can only answer, "You can see for yourself what's coming" — a reply which, instead of relieving, increases Dante's sudden terror.

CHAPTER FIVE
THE CITY OF DIS

In less time than it would take an arrow to run through the air, a little boat speeds through the water of the Marsh of Styx and reaches the shore where Dante and Virgil are waiting. "You are here at last, you wicked soul," the new boatman shouts, looking angrily at Dante. "PHLEGYAS, PHLEGYAS," Virgil answers promptly, "it is useless to shout; we'll be with you only while we pass this mud." All this happens so fast that Dante can hardly look on Phlegyas' face. At Virgil's words the new demon utters no sign of protest but mumbles something that sounds more like anger than resignation. Still master of the situation, Virgil steps down into the boat and tells Dante to do the same. Dante obeys but soon notices that his body has filled the little vessel to capacity. His nerves are on edge, and everything around him is black and weird.

One can hear nothing but the sound of the dead water as the boat cuts through the mysterious blackness of the channel. Looking suspiciously about him, Dante sees now something white, or less black, clinging to one side of the boat and slightly moving: it is a human hand. Someone must be following the boat from underneath. Dante is right, for at this moment a face all covered with mud appears on the surface of the water, asking: "Who are you, who come here before your time?" For the first time Dante defends himself, giving Virgil no time to speak out for him. He replies: "Yes, I am coming, but not to stay. But who are *you,* so vile and dirty?" "Can't you see? I'm one who weeps," says the foul, half-floating soul. Suddenly Dante recognizes him— it is mad FILIPPO ARGENTI of Florence. "And may you weep forever!" says Dante to him, while Virgil, striking on his clutching hand, pushes him away from the boat. Dante himself would perhaps be unable to tell why Argenti's words have infuriated him so much. Is it because for the first time a man from his own town considers him, too, eternally lost?

"Here we are," says Virgil, pointing to several houses in a valley below, all of them looking like mosques lighted for the night. "That is the CITY OF DIS." This entire strange city appears surrounded by walls made of solid, thick iron. Phlegyas takes his two passengers more than once around the forbidding walls until he cries out: "Here is the entrance. Off! Get off!" Virgil and Dante leave the boat; Phlegyas disappears. But where is the entrance? There seems to be no entrance at all.

There are, instead, more than a thousand ghosts looking down from above the gates and angrily shouting: "Who is that man down there, who, still alive, goes through the kingdom of the dead?" As if unconcerned with their number and their threats, Virgil makes a sign of wishing to speak to them privately. "All right then," shout all the thousand ghosts from above the gates, "come in alone, but let the other go. Let him go back alone, for you are going to stay here with us. Send him away."

"O my beloved guide," cries Dante, bewildered, "you, who more than seven times have saved me from danger, do not abandon me now! And if we are not allowed to go farther, let us go back together right away." You can well understand Dante's fear. How could he go back alone? How could he retrace his steps through the Marsh, the dark rain and snow, the Endless Storm, and the walls of Limbo, back to the Dark Forest and the three wild beasts undoubtedly still waiting for him? Now he understands why he grew instinctively afraid at the sight of the two small lights on the tower. This is probably the end of his life—of his body and of his soul. So great is his fear that he seems to have completely forgotten about the Blessed Lady and Beatrice.

"Have no fear," says Virgil, seeing him so frightened, "for nothing and no one can ever say No to God. Wait for me here, and do not let one thought of despair enter your mind, for I won't leave you in this low world." This said, Virgil walks bravely toward the main gate. But how can Dante let no thought of despair enter his mind? His mind is like a battlefield where two armies fight against each other. One thought seems to say: "Yes, everything will be all right." Another thought seems to reply: "No, he won't be back, and you will have to go alone and die on your way."

When he lifts his eyes, he sees Virgil very near the gate of the City of Dis. His heart is beating fast. The gate is still open, waiting for Virgil to enter; but all of a sudden it closes in his face with a sound that is heard throughout the night. Evidently the thousand ghosts have changed their minds and do not wish to talk to Virgil any more. Or is it only one of their evil tricks before they kill them both? Pale and perhaps frightened, Virgil walks slowly back to Dante, saying: "Whatever they do, they cannot win. Someone will come to help us unless..."

Unless what? Unless Beatrice was wrong, or this trip is no longer willed there where what is willed is done? Dante feels like crying, but he only asks this question: "Is it possible for a soul in Limbo ever to come down here?" Virgil replies that he was here once before a long long time ago, but Dante's attention is elsewhere.

On the burning top of the tower three Furies have appeared and are now looking down. They look like women, judging by their faces and manners; but their hair is made of green, coiling snakes. Each of the three Furies is rending her breast with her claws, screaming: "Let Medusa come, and turn that man to stone." Dante knows who Medusa is and what she can do to people: if one but looks at her, one is immediately turned into stone. That is why, wasting no time, Virgil tells Dante to turn back and keep his eyes closed. Dante obeys.

But what is happening now? Has Medusa come? Are the thousand ghosts coming down from above the gates? Has the door been opened again? Are the souls from within the City of Dis marching at the command of the three Furies? Dante does not dare open his eyes. He hears a sudden wind, stronger than the Endless Storm in the Second Circle, which makes both shores tremble, and seems to shake the whole City. "Now you can open your eyes," says Virgil to Dante with a joyous sound in his voice. Dante opens his eyes and sees an Angel from Heaven walking on the Marsh of Styx with feet unwet. How bright he is! Dante notices that the Heavenly Messenger is not accustomed to that darkness, for he often moves his left hand before him to remove the thick, black air from his face. And now that he is closer, one can see that his eyes are full of indignation as if they were saying, "Who is like God?"

As soon as they see the unexpected Angel, the thousand ghosts run in fear inside the City, and the three Furies abandon the burning top of the tower. The Angel goes straight to the gate, opens it with a magic wand at once, and says to those who are hiding in terror inside the iron walls: "How dare you forget that this is willed there where what is willed is never left unfinished?" After these words the Heavenly Messenger goes fast back where he came from, and Virgil and Dante walk into the SIXTH CIRCLE where are punished the HERETICS, those who believe that the soul dies with the body.

Dante does not dare ask Virgil why, in order to come into this City, they had to wait for an Angel from Heaven, and why the old password had no power this time. He will know the answer later. For the time being, he needs to know only this: with the City of Dis begins the second part of Hell, which is far worse than the first. Until now he has met sinners who somehow did not use their intellect in their evil actions. But from now on he will meet people punished with much greater torture and for much greater sins.

But what is this—a graveyard? Each tomb is open and—what is worse—on fire; yet Dante sees not one soul in them.

"Come!" says Virgil, and Dante follows him in silence.

Dante meets Farinata and Cavalcanti.

CHAPTER SIX
TOMBS ON FIRE

After a few steps through those tombs Dante asks Virgil if it would be possible to see the souls lying in them. Dante has no doubt now, that this trip through Hell is really willed in Heaven, and so for the first time he shows no fear. But his courage seems to fade as soon as from one of those open tombs he hears these words: "O man from Florence, stay here awhile. I am the one who defeated your city." From tomb to tomb goes the echo: "Your city . . . your city . . . your city."

Hearing that voice and still seeing no one, Dante gets closer to his guide; but Virgil tells him: "Turn around! There's FARINATA. You can see him from his waist up." Dante turns around and can hardly believe his own eyes. Is that man General Farinata degli Uberti, the man who defeated Florence twice, in 1248 and in 1260?

Dante, who has heard so much about him, stares and stares at him with a mixture of fear and awe. So, that man is Farinata, the father-in-law of Guido Cavalvanti, Dante's best friend, and the ruthless Commander- in-chief responsible for so much bloodshed. Dante had not yet been born at the time of the Battle of Montaperti, but he remembers what he has heard from the few soldiers who did not die in that battle. The battlefield was totally covered with corpses, and the blood of dead soldiers and dead horses was so much that it made the Arbia River red for many days and many nights.

Look at him now, sitting up in his tomb, with flames all about him, but still fierce and terrifying as he was on earth. He seems not to care at all about the very fire that tortures him. Dante is still staring at him, but now Virgil, pushing him toward the tomb, tells him to go and talk to him, and not be afraid.

Looking at Dante a little, Farinata asks him this question: "Did your parents belong to my Party— yes or no?" His voice is so frightening that Dante answers at once: "No, sir. They were Guelphs, not Ghibellines." Raising his eyebrows in scorn and anger, Farinata says: "Well then, let me tell you this:

Twice have I defeated and chased them away."

At this point Dante wonders why this man lives still in the past. Does he not know that the Ghibellines are no longer in power in Florence? As a matter of fact the Guelphs have been at City Hall thirty-four years. Why does he not know this? Strange. Perhaps these souls in Hell cannot know, or are not allowed to know, what goes on in the world. But why did Ciacco in the Third Circle tell him about the future? Who knows, perhaps in Hell one can know the future but not the present.

When he looks at Farinata again, Dante can see how smug he is in the thought of having defeated the Guelphs twice. Yes, he is the ruthless man responsible for so much bloodshed and sorrow. Why does Dante feel sorry for him? Has he not been warned by Virgil not to be afraid of him? All right then, he will defend his own Party, and let him know that the Battle of Montaperti was not the end of Florence after all.

"Yes, I know that you have defeated and chased them away twice," Dante replies to the General, "but the Guelphs have come back both times whereas your Ghibellines are still kept far away from the walls of our City." Imagine the effect of these words on Farinata.

But look, look there, at the next tomb. A fiery shadow is rising from its coffin—it is a man on his knees. He looks around Dante as if to see if someone else is with him; but when he realizes that Dante is alone at the foot of Farinata's tomb, he asks, weeping: "If you have been allowed, for your great intelligence, to come, still alive, into this blind world of the dead, where is my son, and why is he not with you?" Dante recognizes him at once—he is Guido Cavalcanti's father. The poor man does not think at all of the dangers of a journey through Hell; he only knows that his son is so intelligent as to deserve any privilege, any favor. Forgetting all about Farinata still in front of him, and deeply moved by the question of Guido's father, Dante answers: "I am sorry: I did not come of my own will, but am guided by that man over there, whom your Guido was perhaps not very fond of." "What?" cries the poor father at these words, standing up straight in his grave, "did you say *was?* Then, is my son dead? Does not the lovely light still pierce his eyes?"

Now Dante realizes that the souls in Hell do not know the present. They may know the future but certainly they do not know the present. Guido, his best friend, is still alive, and yet his father does not know. That is why not even Farinata is aware of what goes on in Florence these days.

Receiving no immediate answer, and believing Dante's silence to mean only one thing, the poor old man falls on his back and is seen no more.

But all this time Farinata has been thinking about Guelphs and Ghibellines, Ghibellines and Guelphs. He has not even noticed that his neighbor has interrupted his political conversation with Dante. To him the life of his Party is more important than anything else.

"If, as you say," the General continues, "my people are still kept far away from the walls of Florence, this news hurts me more than this bed of fire. In less than four years you too will know what it means to be far from your own City. But tell me: why are you so cruel to my Party?" Dante would like to answer: "Of all people, you should not speak of cruelty. You have been the most cruel of all." But he only says: "Have you forgotten the Arbia River red with Florentine blood?" "No," shouts the General, "I have not forgotten Montaperti. But I was not the only one. I was the only one, though, the only one who defended Florence when everybody else was thinking of destroying her." Dante had never thought of that. Now he knows what must have happened soon after that battle.

Drunken with victory and still thirsty for blood, the Ghibellines had decided to raze Florence to the ground so that she could rise and fight no more. But "Gentlemen," Farinata told them that day, "what you intend to do is against humanity. We are not barbarians but a civilized people. Yesterday we have proved to the other Italian cities that not even the Pope can stop us. But Florence is a great city and must be saved. If you think that you will kill children, old men and women, you are wrong. If you think that you will burn every house and field, you are wrong— and do you know why? Because I, Farinata, will stop you. He who touches Florence, dies." And so Florence was saved by the very man who had defeated her.

Now Dante sees Farinata in a new light. He is not the cruel, ruthless man people think he is, but a General, so to speak, with a heart of gold. And a new thought at this moment crosses Dante's mind: if Farinata had not saved Florence from total destruction, he would not have been born, for his parents, too, would have been killed with all the other helpless citizens of Florence. He owes his life, then, to this General.

"Sir," says Dante, changing the subject, and deeply sorry for having misjudged so great and generous a man, "it seems to me that you can foresee the future, but do not know the present." Sounding no more like a strong military man but like a sad and tired old man, Farinata explains: "We are like those who have imperfect eyesight. We see the things that belong to the future in that distant edge of light which we have lost forever; but when those things leave that edge of light and move toward us, then they become part of our darkness and we cannot see them any more. This means, as you can well understand, that all our knowledge will be dead when, at the end of the world and time, there will be no more future to know."

That is why Guido Cavalcanti's father did not know that his son was still among the living. Dante feels sorry for having given him such a wrong impression by not replying quickly to his question, and begs Farinata to tell the truth to that poor neighbor of his.

Walking back toward Virgil, who has been waiting all this time not far from the General's tomb, Dante remembers Farinata's words about his own future, and is almost crushed by their meaning. Somebody has just told you that in less than four years you will have to leave your country, your family, your friends; and you do not know where you will be forced to live the rest of your life, nor do you know if you will ever be allowed to go back to the place where you were born and see once more the things you love so much. What a sad prophecy!

"Why are you so sad?" Virgil asks Dante, who tells him what he has just heard from Farinata. "When you are in the sweet light of Beatrice, you will know from her the journey of your life."

But at this moment not even the mention of Beatrice can relieve the new sorrow in Dante's heart.

CHAPTER SEVEN
THE BLEEDING BUSH

You must have heard of the MINOTAUR. The Minotaur was a monster with a bull's body and a man's head. When His Horror Minos, whom we have met in the Second Circle, was alive and King of Crete, he was so powerful that he commanded the citizens of Athens to send him every year, as a token of their loyalty, seven boys and seven girls. Those seven boys and seven girls were given as food to the Minotaur, who was kept by the King in a labyrinth of long corridors from which no one could ever find the way out except the King himself. After he was killed by Theseus, the violent Bull was reborn in Hell, and there he is now guarding the entrance to the SEVENTH CIRCLE, which is the place where Violence is punished.

When the Minotaur sees Virgil and Dante, he begins to bite himself furiously, thinking perhaps that someone has come to kill him the second time. But Virgil tells him: "Step aside, Beast! This man is here not to kill you but to see how you groan in your punishment." At these words the monster grows furious, exactly like a bull that, having received the fatal stroke from the torero, cannot run any more but only kicks and kicks with bloody rage. "Quick, quick, run to the entrance while he is so mad: this is your chance," Virgil cries out, and Dante does at once as he is told.

With this trick the two avoid the Minotaur and begin to crawl down into the Seventh Circle. The way down is a steep wall of loose stones which the weight of Dante's feet makes fall, one after the other, into a river of boiling blood running below. That RIVER OF BLOOD is the first of the three sections of this new Circle, and in it are punished the VIOLENT AGAINST THEIR NEIGHBORS.

Virgil and Dante come down at last on a narrow strip of land, but are soon surrounded by a troop of strange creatures half horses and half men, called CENTAURS. They are armed with arrows and their job is to patrol the narrow strip of land and see that no sinner leaves his place in the boiling blood. To Chiron, their chief, Virgil says, with a little change, the powerful password, "It is willed there, where what is willed is done," assuring him that Dante, still alive, has come to the dark valley out of necessity and not for pleasure. Chiron understands and, very considerate indeed, assigns NESSUS, one of his Centaurs, to guide and carry the two visitors across the hot stream. Nessus obeys, and, while bearing them across the waves of boiling blood, points at ALEXANDER THE GREAT and other dictators and rulers, immersed in that never ending blood up to their lashes. Nessus leaves them on the other bank of the river.

Virgil and Dante are now on the threshold of a haunted forest, a thick and ugly forest in which they cannot see one twig that is green. If you expect to smell the freshness of spring you are mistaken, for every single blade of grass is poisoned here. Look— those round things hanging from the branches of the trees are fruits, but do not touch them, for they too are poisoned. You remember all of a sudden that woods and forests on earth have birds that sing sweet songs among the green leaves. But here there are only Harpies.

The HARPIES are strange and monstrous birds with human necks and faces and with wide wings, clawed feet, and large and feathered bellies. Hiding in the trees, they shriek with horrible cries, and their laments are the only living things in this wood of death.

This is the second section of the Seventh Circle, and here are punished the VIOLENT AGAINST THEMSELVES, those who have committed suicide.

Life is God's gift to man, the most precious gift of all. Life, therefore, must be held and handled as a sacred thing until we are asked to give it back to God. One who commits suicide offends not only God, the giver of all life, but also Nature, of which man's life is the greatest and highest beauty. By killing himself, man forgets that only God is the owner of his life. He shows that he is ashamed of being the highest and greatest thing in Nature. All suicides, therefore, are punished even by Nature, which now gives them what they deserve. They are turned into trees and twigs and bushes, thus passing to the inferior vegetable level. In other words, they do not look like human beings any more.

After walking a little through this haunted forest, Dante is asked by Virgil to break off a tiny shoot from one of the bushes in front of him. Dante obeys, but something unbelievable happens. From that very bush comes out a spurt of blood, and soon a voice of pain is heard: "Why do you tear me? Why do you hurt me?" Terrified, Dante drops the little shoot. But blood and words still flow from the broken bush, and the mysterious voice continues: "Why do you tear me? Have you no pity at all? We are trees and bushes now, but once we were men like you. If we were snakes, perhaps your hand would be less cruel." Dante cannot even ask: "Whose voice is this?" But, as always, Virgil understands, and begs the wounded soul to tell his story. The sinner who has spoken from the bleeding bush is PIER DELLA VIGNA.

Pier Della Vigna was a cobbler's son who rose to be Treasurer and Secretary of State to the noble Emperor Frederick II, and then fell by jealousy and treachery. He was so close to the Emperor that people used to say of him that he held both keys to Frederick's heart. But for this he had many enemies among the courtiers, and one day he was accused of treason. Enraged by all the evidence against his Secretary, the Emperor had him arrested, blinded, and thrown into a dungeon. Although his conscience claimed innocence to the last,

Pier committed suicide by banging his head against a wall. This happened in 1249, sixteen years before Dante was born. When Dante was a young man, people still talked about the tragic death of Pier Della Vigna at the Court of Palermo in Sicily. Was he innocent? Was he guilty? No one really knew.

But now Dante hears Pier's sad story from his very lips, and is soon convinced that the poor man is innocent. Pier Della Vigna assures him, first, that it was Envy, the plague of every court, that destroyed him by inflaming all minds against him. Then he explains that he committed suicide because he thought that death alone would free him from disdain. "By the new roots of this tree," he concludes with heart-rending sincerity, "I swear to you, never did I break faith to my Lord, who was so worthy of honor. And if either of you return to the world, please clear my name, which still lies under Envy's crushing weight."

To have his name cleared among men on earth, Pier even tells Virgil and Dante how the souls of the suicides get tangled up in those trees and bushes. All those who kill themselves are immediately sent by Minos to the Seventh Circle. They fall into this forest and no place is chosen for them. Wherever chance flings them, there they sprout and shoot up to a sapling or to a thorny bush. Like all the other dead, on Judgment Day they too will go back on earth looking for their bodies; but, since they will not be allowed to be clothed with them again, they will drag them here, and throughout the haunted forest their bodies will hang forever, each from the tree or bush in which its soul is imprisoned.

The Harpies, hidden in the forest, are waiting for Virgil and Dante to leave, so that once more they may swoop down with fury and sate their hunger, feeding on the leaves that are human limbs.

CHAPTER EIGHT
ON THE BACK OF GERYON

In the third section of the Seventh Circle, which begins at the end of the Haunted Forest, Dante sees a naked plain of BURNING SAND. Here are punished the VIOLENT AGAINST GOD, NATURE, and THE ARTS.

Among those who have done violence against God — they all lie on their backs upon the scorching sand — Dante sees one who does not seem to care at all either about the flames below or the large, thick flakes of fire falling on him. He is CAPANEUS, one of the seven rebellious Kings who defied the gods, especially Jupiter, and were punished by their fatal thunderbolt. Capaneus, who met his death standing, has lost nothing of his ancient arrogance: even in Hell he raises his voice of scorn and defiance against Heaven. Dante understands that Capaneus is punished not for his contempt of the mythological gods as such but for his rebellion to the idea of religion as such. Lying down disdainful and twisted on the burning sand, he must spend his eternity realizing that there is Someone higher and more powerful than man, and that it is foolish of man to challenge the One who created him.

Dante is puzzled. How will he walk across the fiery sand? He cannot see one inch of the plain where he may put his feet without burning them at once; and even if there were a narrow path untouched by the glowing embers, the thick, large flakes of fire raining from above would make a sudden flaming torch of him. But fortunately Virgil tells him: "Now follow me, and see that you do not place your feet upon the burning sand; but always walk along the edge of the wood." Along the edge of the wood they go, until they come to a narrow rivulet the redness of which makes Dante shudder. Springing from the thick of the Haunted Forest, this little red rivulet crosses the Plain of the Burning Sand and has the power of quenching all the flames above it. The two Poets walk along its banks across the fiery desert.

When the edge of the wood comes to an end Dante sees the VIOLENT AGAINST NATURE, the Sodomites. As an old tailor squints at the eye of his needle, so each of these new sinners stares and stares at Dante, wondering who he may be.

Dante is immediately recognized by BRUNETTO LATINI, who, leaving his own group, begs him to let him walk a little by his side, explaining to him that, should he stop for only one minute, he would have then to lie a hundred years without being allowed to brush off the striking rain of fire.

Poor Ser Brunetto! Dante cannot help feel sorry for the dear and kind old man who on earth used to teach him what man must do to make himself immortal. He wants him to know that he is still grateful to him, and that nothing will ever make him less fond of him. The two men are as happy to see each other again as they are embarrassed. Brunetto Latini is embarrassed to be found in Hell, and in such a place, by his young student and friend. And Dante, too, is embarrassed when he has to confess to his teacher, who had always thought very highly of him, that, though still alive, he too is dead, being in mortal sin, and his unusual journey is no reward at all but the one alternative left for his salvation.

But so great is the affection between the two that each tries to make the other think of only happy things. Even when Brunetto tells Dante about his future sufferings at the hands of his enemies, he softens the harshness of his prophecy by assuring him that he will also be much honored. Remembering Farinata's words ("In less than four years you too will know what it means to be far from your own City"), Dante answers: "This much I would have you know: I am quite ready to face the change of Fortune." But he does not want to impress Ser Brunetto with his sudden courage; he only wants to assure him that his words of encouragement and his unchanged belief in him have strengthened his soul once more as in the good old days on earth. And as in the good old days on earth, once again Brunetto Latini mentions his own book, called *Treasure,* of which he was, and is still, so proud. But Dante senses something else in Brunetto's last words, "Remember my *Treasure,* in which I still live." He is sure that the dear old man meant only this: "Forget how and where you have seen me last; remember me not as a soul forever lost but as a spirit still living in the best of what I gave to the world." And, oh, how it grieves Dante's heart to see the kindest friend of his youth run, at the glimpse of a new smoke rising from the sand, to join his sad companions.

Virgil and Dante hear at this point the sound of a waterfall. It is the water that plunges down into the Eighth Circle. But before they reach that place, which seems the only possible entrance to the new Circle, three more shadows come close to them. Dante meets three Florentines of great distinction— IACOPO RUSTICUCCI, GUIDO GUERRA, and TEGGHIAJO ALDOBRANDI, who, in turn, recognizing Dante's Florentine garment, ask the unexpected visitor about their beloved City. Replying to them with great respect, Dante tells them that Florence, their sweet land, has become a nest of pride and abuses, and is already weeping because of it. "If you get out of these dark regions and see again the beautiful stars," say those three, before making wings of their legs, "please remember us to the people up there." This is not the first time that a soul in Hell has asked to be remembered among the living. There seems to be still a link between life and death, time and eternity, and it is exactly this link of human understanding and affection that once more explains to Dante and to us the difference between sin and sinner.

But here is the reddish waterfall over a cliff. Its sound deafens Dante's ears. "Give me your belt," says Virgil to Dante, who, not knowing what his Guide intends to do with it, hands it to him coiled and wound up. Incidentally, Dante had thought of using this belt of his to catch the Leopard in the Dark Forest, which perhaps he would have done if the sudden appearance of the Lion had not frozen him with fear. But what is Virgil going to do with it? What can one do with a little belt on the brink of so deep a cliff? Virgil throws it down into the abyss, without saying a word, but sure that something will come of it. And something does come of it.

If you have a weak heart, don't look down, for something is coming up from below that will astonish the most courageous soul. Through the thick, dark air a monstrous shape comes swimming, swimming up, like one returning to the surface after loosening an anchor from a rock or some other object down at the bottom of the sea.

"Here is the Beast with the sharp tail, who passes mountains, breaks through walls and weapons, and fills the whole world with his stench." This said, Virgil signals the savage monster to come ashore near the end of the rocky path; and the Beast obeys, landing with his head and breast on the cliff but keeping his tail hanging in the void. He is so huge that no detail of his body is lost to Dante's sight.

His face is the face of a righteous man, but the rest of his body is that of a serpent. His two paws are hairy to the armpits; his back and breast, and both his flanks, are as if painted with knots and circlets of infinite colors. His tail, like that of an enormous scorpion, hangs in the hollow of the abyss with its poisonous fork twisting and writhing at its tip.

"While I talk to this Beast," says Virgil to Dante, pointing to some people sitting near the cliff, "take a last look at this place so that you may miss nothing of this section. Go, and talk to them awhile." Dante knows what Virgil is going to say to the Beast. He is going to use once more, as he has done so far at the entrance to each new Circle, the mighty password, "It is willed there, where what is willed is done." But why is he sending him away? Is Virgil afraid that the monster might behave like that legion of ghosts above the gates of the City of Dis? Or does he really want Dante not to miss a thing of the section they are about to leave forever? With these thoughts Dante walks all alone toward the souls sitting sadly on the brink of the precipice.

They are the VIOLENT AGAINST THE ARTS, or the Usurers. Usurers are those who lend money at an excessive amount of interest. But why are they called Violent Against the Arts? According to Dante, Nature is the Child of God, and human industry, which tries to imitate Nature, is Art. Art, therefore, is the Grandchild of God. But by distorting the means and purposes of his imitation of productive Nature, a usurer does violence to the very art or craft he employs, and loses sight of what he intends to imitate. That is why all these sinners are punished as they are.

Their grief is bursting forth through their eyes, and with their hands, in constant movement, they try to brush off now the flames and now the specks of the burning sand. They make Dante think of what a dog does when bitten by fleas or flies in the heat of summer.

He fails to recognize any of them, so baked are their features. But he sees a purse hanging from the neck of each of them, and on every purse, which shows a certain color and a certain design like a coat of arms, two eyes are eagerly feasting. These sinners are all Florentines except one who is from Padua. When this one turns to Dante, shouting, "What are you doing in this pit? Get out," Dante goes back to Virgil and the horrid Beast.

But there is Virgil, already mounted on the back of the weird monster. "Now be bold," he says to Dante, "jump up and sit in front of me so that the tail may not harm you." At these words Dante feels an icy shudder through his spine, but Virgil looks at him sternly as if to say: "What is this fear? Have you still any doubt in the power of Heaven after all you have seen and heard?" Feeling ashamed of himself, Dante mounts the monster and sits in front of his Guide. He does not utter a word, but would like to say: "At least hold me tight!" Reading his thought, Virgil clasps him with his arms and then calls out: "Now let's go, Geryon! Move slow and steady down, and bear in mind you are carrying a living man."

GERYON! Only now Dante seems to understand every detail of the enormous creature. His other name is Fraud. Geryon has the face of a righteous man because fraudulent people seem good and trustworthy. His paws are hairy to the armpits because the deeds of a fraudulent man are well hidden and disguised in their beginning. His back and breast, and both his flanks, are as if painted with knots and circlets of infinite colors because fraudulent people conceal their malice under a thousand entanglements of false brightness and cheerfulness. And the extremity of his body is sharp and poisonous because only at the end do fraudulent people reveal the damage of their actions.

Everything is clear now. On the rump of Fraud itself Virgil and Dante are now descending into the Lower Hell, where the Fraudulent are punished.

Circling and moving down as a falcon, Geryon touches at last the bottom of the abyss and, when free of his weight, fades out of sight as fast as an arrow.

On the back of Geryon.

CHAPTER NINE
A POPE TURNED UPSIDE DOWN

The EIGHTH CIRCLE, made of ten EVIL POCKETS, is the place of Simple Fraud whereas the Ninth will be the place of Complex Fraud. The ten Evil Pockets, called MALEBOLGE, resemble the trenches which surround a fortress, and contain different classes of sinners or, rather, different groups of fraudulent sinners. Little, narrow bridges made of gray stone run from one pit to the other, and make Dante think of roads leading from different directions into a fortified castle.

In the FIRST EVIL POCKET are punished the SEDUCERS and PANDERERS. Though forming two separate crowds, they all are naked, and Horned Demons hurry them along with the fierceness of their scourges.

In the SECOND EVIL POCKET are punished the FLATTERERS. Puffing with their mouths and nostrils, and hitting themselves with open hands, they are fully dipped in excrement, which seems to have flowed there from all the sewers on earth.

But it is the THIRD EVIL POCKET that arouses Dante's indignation for the first time in this part of the Lower Hell. When along the sides and bottom of the new abyss he sees many narrow holes, all round and of one size, with two quivering legs aflame coming out of each of them, he knows who these new sinners are. They are the SIMONIACS, those who, following the evil example of Simon the Sorcerer who tried to buy from the Apostle Peter the power to give the HolyGhost, make of the things of God a filthy market to enrich their own pockets with silver and gold.

How great is Divine Wisdom! God had created them with head and eyes that should have looked to the sky for the vision of high and divine beauty; and now the same God punishes them for having used head and eyes for the contemplation of low and vile things of earth. They lived as if their feet were up and their heads down, and so are they punished here in Hell.

Each Simoniac occupies a round narrow hole, buried upside down, his head and bust in the ground and completely invisible, and only his legs and feet showing out of the hole. An oily flame burns and devours, without ever wasting, the soles of his feet, and such is the furious quivering of the joints that they would snap and break to pieces cords or ropes of every kind and size.

Dante knows that this is the place where unworthy Popes and Cardinals, Bishops and Priests, pay for the crime of turning the House of God into a den of thieves. By now he has learned the difference between sin and sinner, yet in the presence of these particular sinners not one feeling of human pity moves his heart. How can he feel sorry for people who, instead of saving the souls entrusted to their care, corrupted them with the example of their greed? They are those who curse the good and bless the wicked, contrary to every teaching of Christ. They are those who fill the world with the putrid smell of their actions, instead of cleansing it with the fragrance of their holiness. They are those who know what is good and sacred, yet trample on it. No, Dante cannot feel sorry for them. He has at this moment a particular man in mind, one who is still alive but who should already be here in one of these holes—Pope Boniface VIII. How well Dante knows Pope Boniface, though he has never yet met him. Instead of devoting his time and energies to the things of God, what does Pope Boniface think of? He has his eyes on Florence and keeps his finger in every political intrigue, stirring up animosities and leaving no stone unturned to achieve wealth and power. He has even thought of a Holy Year now, but why? Probably to prove to the world and the Emperor how powerful he is and even to increase the "Treasure of Saint Peter." How well Dante knows Pope Boniface. And now that he remembers the predictions of Ciacco, Farinata, and Brunetto Latini, he feels sure that Pope Boniface will be the one responsible for the new bloodshed in Florence and for his own sufferings.

All these thoughts are storming in Dante's mind when suddenly he sees two legs thrusting from a hole, mercilessly sucked by a stronger, ruddier flame. "Master," he asks Virgil, "who is that one, writhing and quivering more than the others?" "If you want me to carry you down there," replies Virgil, "he himself will tell you who he is and why he is there." "I like what you like," says Dante, "for you read my every thought."

The way down is so steep that even a goat would find it a hard and painful passage. But Virgil carries Dante down the slope with great ease and tenderness, and, only when they reach that special hole, puts him down.

Wasting no time, Dante bends over the hole and asks, "Whoever you are, wretched soul, planted like a stake with your head down and your feet up, talk to me if you can." At these words the soul cries out from the bottom of his grave: "Are you there already, are you there already, Boniface? I did not expect you here so soon . . ." Other words of scorn come out of the hole, but Dante, baffled by what he has heard, does not know what to answer. "Answer: 'I am not the one, I am not the one you think,'" says Virgil then. So Dante answers.

Harshly disappointed, the buried sinner twists his feet in anger and says with tearful voice: "What, then, do you want from me? If to know who I am has made you come so deep to this cliff, then let me tell you that the Pope's mantle was once upon my shoulders. Truly was I a son of the She-Bear, so eager to enrich my little cubs that I pursed wealth on earth and myself down here."

Pope NICHOLAS III! At last Dante knows who this sinner is. He was once Giovanni Caetano Orsini, and "Orsini" means "bear cubs" in Italian.

Pope Nicholas III, a born politician, died when Dante was only fifteen years old. He bestowed so many titles and so much wealth on his nephews and the other members of his family that no one doubted that the Orsini family meant much more to him than the Church itself.

His indignation growing, Dante, still bent over the hole, lets the former Pope talk. Nicholas tells him that beneath his head, cowering through the fissures of the rock, are the others who preceded him in the sin of simony, and that he too will fall down when Pope Boniface comes to occupy his place, and then the same thing will happen to Boniface when the next Pope arrives, and so on.

But at this point Dante's anger explodes. Not so much the thought of the past as of the future simony wounds him now. Why should all this happen in the Church of God? Why have all these Popes forgotten the poverty of Christ and of the first Apostles? Why can they not understand that material wealth is the seed of all corruption? Why can they fail to see that, when it did not have its temporal power, the Church was really the chaste Bride of Christ? Have these Popes or Pastors read the Gospel they are supposed to know and teach to others?

"Tell me now," Dante asks Pope Nicholas with sorrow and sarcasm in his voice, "how much cash our Lord asked of Saint Peter before He put the Keys of the Kingdom into his keeping. He asked nothing but 'Follow me.' Nor did Peter, or the others, ask gold or silver of Matthias when they chose him for the place that Judas, the wicked apostle, had lost. So stay where you are. and in this hole where you belong keep a good watch on your filthy money. Dante realizes now that he is being a bit too rash. After all, this sinner was once a Pope. "And were it not for the reverence I have for the Great Keys which you held on earth," he continues, "I would use much heavier words . . . You have made yourself a god of gold and silver; and what is the difference between you and a pagan, save that he worships one, and you a hundred idols?"

Dante would like to say more, so great still is his indignation. But it is no use preaching to one who can no longer repent of the evil done. If he at least could see the Pope's face now! But he might guess by the mad anger of those two feet kicking in mid-air furiously and in vain.

All this while, Virgil has listened to Dante's words with a satisfied look on his face. He is indeed pleased with his "son," seeing how great a concept of religion he has in his mind. For the first time he has seen him act and talk like a courageous man. Now he knows that his suggestion of this journey through Hell was a good one. The man in his charge is learning. When they leave the darkness of this pit to see the stars once more, Beatrice will be proud of his guidance.

At this point Virgil lifts Dante with both arms and, holding him tight to his chest, climbs the difficult slope up to the rocky bridge. When he puts him down on it the FOURTH EVIL POCKET is already within sight.

CHAPTER TEN
INFERNAL FOLLY

The Fourth Evil Pocket shows at its bottom people moving silent and weeping. As he takes a better look at them, Dante sees them horribly disfigured, with their faces completely turned on their necks, so they could only look backward, with tears streaming not on their chests but on their buttocks.

Seeing man's image so twisted, Dante begins to weep, leaning on one of the rocks of the steep cliff. But Virgil rebukes him, saying: "Are you, too, like the other fools? Who is more wicked than those who with their tears would like to make God's justice seem injustice? Lift up your eyes, and see who they are."

When Dante hears, among a few others, the names of TIRESIAS and MICHAEL SCOTT, he understands that these new sinners are the FORTUNETELLERS and SORCERERS. They are punished as they are because on earth they thought themselves capable of understanding the things which God had denied to man's knowledge, and the more they tried to know what lay ahead the more they discovered what was behind, thus being brought far away from the effect they wanted to achieve.

On earth the moon is now setting on the morning of Holy Saturday, and Virgil knows why they must hasten to the next Pocket.

The FIFTH EVIL POCKET contains the POLITICAL GRAFTERS, those who for the sake of easy money take advantage of their authority or public trust, and say Yes for No and No for Yes. They are sunk in sticky boiling pitch where they are constantly bobbing up and down. Dante sees no sinners but only bubbles raised by the boiling. He is still looking down into that weird enormous pot when, "Watch out! Watch out!" says Virgil, pulling him from the place where he has been standing. Frightened, Dante turns around and sees a black Demon who arrives from the earth with a SENATOR OF LUCCA on his shoulders, dumps him into the BOILING PITCH from the top of the bridge, and flies back to the world of the living to grab his next political grafter. As the newly arrived sinner falls with a splash into the pitch, a throng of Demons with hooks and pitchforks jump with more than a hundred weapons, saying: "Dance all alone down there, and see what you can grab now that no one checks on you." This said, they do to him what one in the kitchen does with a fork to a piece of meat in order to keep it deep in the stew. "Now, you, hide behind this crag," says Virgil to Dante, "while I go down to talk to them, and do not be afraid, for nothing can happen to me, who have been through all this already." Dante recalls at these words their experience at the gate of the City of Dis and, thinking of the sudden protection from Heaven, crouches behind a rock with hope in his heart.

But as soon as the armed Demons catch a glimpse of Virgil coming down the slope from the top of the bridge, they raise their hooks against him, like dogs madly rushing upon a poor old beggar who stops in front of a house to ask for food. Calm and unafraid, "Wait," cries Virgil to them. "Before your pitchforks touch me, send one of you here, for I want to talk to him." The Demons send Evil Tail as their ambassador. "Do you think, Evil Tail," says Virgil, "I could have come here free from harm without protection from above? You, too, must let me go on, for it is willed in Heaven that I show someone this savage road." At the magic password Evil Tail drops his hook and shouts to his fellow Demons: "Stop! Don't harm him!" At a signal from Virgil Dante comes out of his hiding place and rushes down the slope to his protector's side. Seeing a living man in their midst, the Demons surround him, grinding their teeth and waiting to raise their hooks and grapples. Getting closer and closer, one of them asks with a leer: "May I just pat him on the back?" But Evil Tail stops him, saying: "Quiet, quiet, Big Tough!" Then, assuring Virgil that he and his charge will find a grotto leading into the next den, he chooses ten of his devils to escort the two visitors along the edge of the boiling pitch.

Dante does not seem to trust this ugly company, for he says to Virgil: "Master, if you know the way, let us go alone." But Virgil answers: "Let them grind their teeth, for it is not for us but for the wretches in the pocket." The ten Demons are walking ahead of Virgil and Dante, and for a while nothing can be heard but the grinding of their teeth. Dante tries to remember their names: LIMP WING, TRAMPLE FROST, MAD DOG, CURLY BEARD, LUSTY EGG, DRAGON-FACE, PIG TUSK, DOG SCRATCHER, WICKED BIRD, and CRAZY RED.

Evil Tail has warned the ten that no harm should come to their two guests; but what if they should disobey their Chief? The boiling pitch is hardly two steps away. If Virgil were not beside him, Dante would probably call this moment his last.

The short silence is broken by a strange noise, made by one of the escorting Demons not with his mouth or with his feet or hands, but you may guess with what part of his body. It is their signal: the weirdest game is about to begin for the amusement of the two guests.

You must have seen how porpoises leap and leap around a ship to warn the sailors (such is the popular belief) of an impending storm. In the same way at this moment some of the grafters, to ease their pain, leap out of the boiling pitch and plunge down again. Many others, also to ease their suffering, are squatting along the bank of the pond like frogs resting on the edge of a ditch with their muzzles out and their legs and bodies deep in the water.

As soon as they see Curly Beard coming with the other Demons, the sinners jump fast into the pitch one after the other. But one of them, not so fast as he would like to be, does not make it, and falls instead under Dog Scratcher's grappling hook, which drags the sinner up in the air, dripping like an otter. Before the devilish fun begins, Dante begs Virgil to ask the wretch who he is. He is CIAMPOLO, once a famous courtier and grafter at the Court of Thibaut II, King of Navarre. But the Demons do not want to wait one minute longer.

Pig Tusk, the demon who shows a menacing tusk on either side of his cavernous mouth, gets close to Ciampolo, hooked by his tar-clotted hair, and gives a piece of his mind with a rip from one of his tusks. But Curly Beard, the appointed Chief of the Ten, has a better idea. Locking him in his arms, he says: "Don't you dare take him away from me. Wait till I pierce him through with my pitchfork." "We have waited long enough," shouts Lusty Egg, who, to prove his impatience, grapples Ciampolo's arm with his hook and, there, rips off a piece of it. Dragonface, too, wants to show that he has an idea of his own by a catch at Ciampolo's legs. Curly Beard, enraged by the intrusion, and feeling robbed of his role in the game, keeps the two demons at a distance, and shouts: "Stay off," when he sees Wicked Bird rolling his eyes to strike.

But Ciampolo, who was not a politician for nothing, has meanwhile thought of a plan to save himself from Curly Beard's pitchfork. If it works out, he will have outsmarted not one but ten devils; if it does not, too bad.

"If you care to see or hear Tuscans or Lombards," he says, "I will make them come out of the pitch. But promise me not to be too close with those evil claws of yours, so that they may not be afraid of their ripping; and I, sitting right here, shall whistle and call seven of them out of the pond. How's that?" Raising his snout at these words, Mad Dog says with a sneer: "Isn't this fellow shrewd? What a nice thing to think of to throw himself into the pitch." "I'm shrewd indeed," retorts Ciampolo, not giving up, "especially when I can think of greater punishment for my fellow sinners." Nine out of ten devils decide not to trust the Navarrese, but Limp Wing takes up Ciampolo's challenge, saying: "All right then; but if you try to jump down from the top of that rock I will beat my wings above the pitch before you even reach the pond from where you are now." This said, Limp Wing flies up to the top of the rock, followed by the eyes of the other nine demons; but Ciampolo, catching them off guard, and not waiting for their signal, in a flash leaps from the bank into the boiling pitch and saves himself beneath the surface.

Flapping his wings, Limp Wing swoops after him, crying, "You're caught." But his wings are unable to outspeed Ciampolo's terror. This time the falcon cannot catch the duck. At this point Trample Frost, outraged by Ciampolo's trick and, more, by Limp Wing's stupid challenge, grabs Limp Wing in mid-air and madly fights with him. Clawing and tearing each other, the two Demons wrestle with all their fury like two huge bats in the deep of the night, until, with a splash, they both fall into the boiling pond. The heat of the pitch is the one referee who succeeds in separating them; but so sticky and heavy are now their wings that, the harder they try to get out, the deeper they go down. To rescue them, Curly Beard sends four of his boys to the other side of the pond, while the others try from this side to free them with the help of their hooks.

Taking advantage of this moment of confusion, Virgil and Dante walk quietly away.

Dante thinks of a fable which he had learned as a child at the school of his first teacher, Romano. It was the fable of a mouse, a frog, and an eagle. But he does not know that, in less than four years, he too will be accused of graft by his political enemies, and that, on such unjust and cruel charge, he will be banished from his beloved Florence, the sweet city of his childhood.

But what will happen now? Who can be so naive as to think that the ten Demons, so scorned and wounded in their pride, will not chase the two visitors and make Dante pay for their humiliation?

CHAPTER ELEVEN
THE STORY OF A SHIPWRECK

Seeing the Evil Claws flying behind them on wings outstretched, Virgil takes Dante in his arms at once and slides down the next slope. He does with Dante what a mother, awakened by the noise of flames enveloping her house, does with her little child: she clasps him to her breast and runs to safety, thinking more of him than of herself. There on the summit of the rock they are already, the ten ugly enemies, when God's High Providence stops them from swooping down. Thus Virgil and Dante are safe on the brink of the new den.

This is the SIXTH EVIL POCKET where the HYPOCRITES are punished. These sinners wear heavy, leaden cloaks with hoods down to their noses. But their cloaks are gilded outside and dazzle the eyes that look at them. Dante understands at once how just their punishment is. To achieve what they want, the hypocrites color their words and actions, and make themselves brilliant and dazzling to the eyes of those they intend to damage. They seem good and honest, but are not what they seem. So even here in Hell they seem but are not what they seem, for under the shining color of their cloaks there is the heavy, dark, crushing reality of lead.

Dante asks two of these new, slow-walking sinners to tell him who they are and what they have done, when he sees a man crucified by three stakes on the floor of the narrow road in such a position that, to pass on, every sinner has to trample on him. He is CAIAPHAS, the one who counseled the Pharisees to crucify Jesus.

Virgil asks one of the Hypocrites how to get out of the Pocket, and, somewhat disturbed by discovering that Evil Tail has lied to him about the exit, leaves the Sixth Pocket in great haste with Dante following close behind.

They find themselves at the bottom of a cliff, and the only way to reach the next class of sinners is to climb a steep, nearly impossible slope. Seeing his Guide still disturbed and pensive, and thinking of some impending danger, Dante does not say a word but his courage leaves him once again. With a sudden smile Virgil turns to him, thus telling him not to fear. He lifts him in his arms and, slowly, from stone to stone, from gorge to gorge, helps him up to the summit of the chasm. They make it, but Dante falls, exhausted and out of breath, as soon as he reaches the last rock. Rebuked by Virgil for his lack of strength, he rises at once and, pretending not to be tired and afraid any longer, says to him: "Go on, for I am strong and bold." So they start their way down the next slope from the center of the bridge, and finally reach the new den below.

The SEVENTH EVIL POCKET contains the THIEVES. You must have

heard of the infinite varieties and sizes of poisonous serpents which are found in the deserts of Libya or in the forests of Ethiopia. But they are harmless compared to those which punish the Thieves in this Pocket. These sinners' hands, which were untied and agile on earth, now are bound on their backs with knots made of hissing snakes, which, thrusting heads and tails through their loins, fall in front of them in one enormous bundle of horror. Other serpents fly through the air. One of these, before Dante's very eyes, flings itself at one of the sinners, wounding him between neck and shoulder. In less time than it takes you to write *i* or *o* on a page, the wounded thief catches fire, burns, drops down in a heap of ashes; and soon those ashes rise by themselves and resume the sinner's former shape. O Power of God! Who can that sinner be? He must have been an unusual thief on earth to deserve such an unusual distinction in Hell. He is VANNI FUCCI of Pistoia, the one who in 1293 stole the Treasure of San Jacopo from the Church of San Zeno, a man of blood and rage indeed. After he committed his sacrilegious theft with two accomplices, he ran away like the snake that he was, and let an innocent man pay for his crime. But in this den he has to deal with more powerful snakes than he ever was.

Enraged for having been asked to reveal his name, and ashamed at being found in this part of Hell, Vanni Fucci takes his venomous revenge by telling Dante that soon, very soon, every White will be wounded by the Blacks just as he has been wounded by the flying serpent. He concludes his prophecy with such a horrid gesture of blasphemy against God that instantly the snakes take hold of him, choking him and his obscenity. With the bitter remembrance of this brute from Pistoia and of other notorious thieves from Florence, Dante remounts the slope, helped once again by his Guide. Now from the bridge he sees the next chasm, gaping below.

In the EIGHTH EVIL POCKET are trapped those who on earth trapped others— the EVIL COUNSELORS. The darkness down the valley seems different somehow, and even less frightening. It is pierced with thousands and thousands of little sparks floating about, which make Dante think not of stars but of fireflies flitting along a valley on a peaceful summer evening. He is so taken by the unexpected sight that he hardly seems to realize how dangerous it is to lean out from the edge of the bridge. But one of those sparks seems different from all the others— it looks bigger and brighter. Dante knows that every spark conceals and punishes a sinner; but who can the one in that special spark be? It seems now much closer than the others, so close that Dante can clearly see that it is two sparks in one.

When Dante hears from Virgil that in that double-pointed spark are punished the souls of ULYSSES and DIOMEDE, he understands why the two should be there and still together. He remembers in a flash Ulysses' three major feats of evil counseling on earth.

It was he, Ulysses, who stole the Palladium, a statue of Pallas without which, according to an old belief, the Trojans could never win. It was he, Ulysses, who convinced Achilles to go to war, thus breaking Deidamia's heart, much in love with the swift-footed hero. And it was he, Ulysses, who conceived the treacherous plan of the Wooden Horse. But had he not been punished enough by the gods already? Or is he guilty of some greater sin completely unknown to men on earth?

Dante is so eager to talk to him that, understanding and even praising his request, Virgil assures him that his wish will soon be granted; but he, Virgil, must do the talking. In his eagerness to hear a famous man of ancient Greece tell the story of his life and death in his own words, Dante does not even ask himself why this time it is Virgil who wants to deal with a soul in Hell.

Entreated by the Poet of victorious Rome, the double-pointed flame stops in front of Dante. Asked then to speak, without a moment of hesitation it begins to do so. Look— the flame shakes wildly as if struggling with a sudden wind, and its sharper point gives forth a sound which soon becomes a man's voice. It is Ulysses himself speaking, and what he tells Virgil and Dante is a magnificent story of victory and defeat.

It is true that, after ten long years of suffering from sea to sea, Ulysses reached Ithaca, his native rocky island. But it is not true that he lived there happily ever after with his wife Penelope, his son Telemachus, and his father Laertes. How could a man like him find happiness in the monotonous life of a little island, far away from the rest of the world? Yes, poor faithful Penelope was entitled to some years of happy married life after so much waiting and weaving. Yes, his proud son was always around him, eager to hear of wars and heroes. But it was no life at all to reminisce and not to act. He was no longer alive if to those around him he was nothing but the remembrance of a past. He was only a prisoner in his own family, and therefore neither what he was nor what he wanted to be. A man must be his own future. A true man is that something in him which tells him what to do and how to do it— nothing else. Now something stronger than any love of family was telling him that he was not born for the easy, comfortable life of a little king in a little island. He had to travel, he had to know what lay beyond the open sea, beyond the very sun. Athens and Troy were not the whole world, nor could Achilles and Hector have been the only heroes on earth. He had to cross the Pillars of Hercules, he had to see new lands, new men— but why? Because he simply had to.

So, one day, with a single ship and with a few brave men who still believed in him, Ulysses left Ithaca and sailed north. They were not young any more and, by the time they reached the Straits of Gibraltar, they were tired and afraid. He too was tired, but if it is human to grow afraid of the unknown that lies ahead, it is only for the gods to brave every difficulty and overcome every fear. They were facing the Atlantic now — the mysterious and forbidden Atlantic never crossed by man before.

"Brothers in daring," he said to his crew, "who through a hundred thousand dangers have reached the West already, will you give up now, now that the unpeopled world beyond the sun is only one more effort ahead? Remember who you are: "You were not born to live like brutes, but to gain knowledge and pursue virtue.""

That's all Ulysses said to his shipmates, but how he said it no one knows, for something happened at those words. "Sail on! Sail on!" Everybody was young again, and in love with the sea and its beautiful danger. Who had dared say that no man should cross the Pillars of Hercules? Not even the gods could stop them now. Turning the stern of their ship toward morning, winds or no winds, they entered the Atlantic, making wings of the oars.

And on and on for five long months they sailed until Ulysses sighted, dim in the distance, a mountain peak so tall that no one had ever seen the like. "Land!" he shouted to his crew. "Land! Land! Land!" re-echoed the crew with one thundering cry of joy.

What happened next was a matter of seconds. From the strange mountain a storm came, which suddenly struck the forepart of the ship. The ship whirled round three times with all the waters; at the fourth, the poop rose and the prow plunged, until, "as pleased Another," the sea closed over them as the lid on a coffin.

Thus ends Ulysses' own story. Not even Dante knows at this moment that the land sighted by Ulysses and his crew was the Mountain of Purgatory. But he understands the meaning of those three words, "As pleased Another." It was God who stopped Ulysses. But is God against man's desire to pursue knowledge and virtue? No. He wants man to be brave and noble, but through grace and divine help, not through rebellion and self-destruction.

Having told its story, the double-pointed flame seems to lose its light, so quiet it becomes. When Virgil gives it permission to go, Ulysses' flame joins the other sparks of the valley. Ancient Greece has once more bowed to sovereign Rome.

CHAPTER TWELVE
THE WALKING HORRORS

There is a region, in Southern Italy, now called Puglia and in ancient times known as Apulia. It is always scorched by a wrathful sun, and its tallest mountain, called Gargano, is barren and veined with reddish streaks as of coagulated blood. It is the "fateful" region of Italy for on its soil, more than in any other part of the Peninsula, the bloodiest wars and battles were fought through the centuries. At the Battle of Cannae alone, in the Second Punic War, so many Roman soldiers were killed that, as the great historian Livy tells us, Hannibal, to prove the greatness of his victory, boastfully produced before the Senate of Carthage three bushels of gold rings taken from their fingers. Imagine now all the blood from all the wars and battles fought in that region, and you have a faint notion of the blood that flows in the Ninth Evil POCKET.

The NINTH EVIL POCKET is the dwelling place for the SOWERS OF SCANDAL AND SCHISM, those who by the falseness of their doctrines or the malice of their deeds stir up confusion in religion, in politics, and among kinsmen.

A Devil is at the entrance of this new Evil Pocket, and his pleasant task is to split each sinner with his untiring sword. Horribly maimed by that Devil, each sinner goes then, bleeding and dragging the hanging parts of his body, from one end of the Pocket to the other, to return, when his wounds have healed, to the same Devil and the same sword over and over again.

It is impossible for Dante to recognize any of these sinners, so disfigured are they in all their limbs. But some of them will undoubtedly introduce themselves. This is one of the worst, most frightening moments in Dante's journey.

Completely split from chin to buttocks, a man is dragging himself on, his entrails hanging between his legs. Seeing Dante staring at him, he opens his chest with his own hands to show the depth and length of the cut, and says to Dante: "Take a good look at me, and see how Mahomet is mangled." But MAHOMET is not the only walking horror in this Pocket, for all the others are in one way or another split open in this part of Hell. On earth they all spread discord and disunity among men, and so now they must experience in themselves disunity and discord.

Other sinners introduce themselves to Dante when they hear that he is still alive and will go back to earth. Some show their throats pierced through and their noses cut off up to the eyebrows; others, like that CURIO who advised Caesar to cross the Rubicon, show their tongues totally slit; others, like that MOSCA DE' LAMBERTI whose evil proposal was responsible for the bloody enmity between the Ghibellines and Guelphs of Florence, raise through the black air the blood-dripping stumps of their severed arms.

But something much more horrible than all this frightens Dante at this moment. He sees a body without a head coming slowly toward him: who or what can that be? It is a sinner holding by the hair his own severed head, which he swings in his hand like a lantern, thus making a lamp of it to light the narrow path ahead. They are two in one, and one in two.

When this new walking horror reaches the foot of the bridge, Virgil and Dante see the sinner lift his arm up high, with all the head, to make sure that they hear what he has to say to them. Held aloft in front of the two visitors, the sinner's head says: "You who, still alive, are visiting the dead, look at my punishment, and see if there is one as great as this. And so that you may speak of me on earth, I want you to know that I am BERTRAN DE BORN, he who gave ill counsel to the Young King. I put father against son . . . and, because I made two of those who were one, I carry my head divided from my trunk. One sees in me the law of retribution." Dante's eyes are filled with tears. Once

The Thieves

53

more he has seen man's image disfigured beyond possibility of identification. In the case of Bertran de Born, he cannot forget how much he used to admire the poetry of the great Troubadour. Oh, why did he have to give ill advice to Prince Henry, son of Henry II, King of England?

"Why are you still staring?" asks Virgil at this point. "This Pocket is twenty-two miles wide, and you cannot possibly see all the sinners in it. We have to hasten for it must be now one o'clock of Saturday afternoon up on earth." So Dante and Virgil leave the valley of the Sowers of Scandal and Schism, talking about GERI DEL BELLO, a cousin of Dante's own father, sighted by Virgil alone among the last shadows.

Now you should think of all the patients in all the hospitals of the world to be able to imagine the wailings and laments of the souls in the TENTH EVIL POCKET, the last of the Eighth Circle of Hell. They are the FALSIFIERS, those who on earth forge things, or deeds, or words, for the success of their evil schemes. The three classes of these new sinners —FALSIFIERS OF THINGS, FALSIFIERS OF DEEDS, and FALSI- FIERS OF WORD — are all punished in the same way, with countless diseases. All their senses are infected — sight, hearing, smell, touch, and taste. Their ears are eternally deafened by their own lamentations; their nostrils are offended by the stench coming from the huge mounds of putrid flesh about them; their hands are constantly scratching this or that part of their bodies to relieve the great fury of the itch that afflicts them; and their tongues stick out, waiting in vain for one little drop of water.

Among these souls Dante sees GIANNI SCHICCHI of Florence, the one who impersonated dead Buoso Donati to dictate a will in favor of the latter's son Simone.

At last the two Poets leave the Eighth Circle. What next? LUCIFER himself dwells in the Ninth, also called the CENTRAL PIT. What will happen in the presence of Satan? Will their password work? And what was the meaning of those strange words *("Pape Satan, Pape Satan aleppe"),* uttered by Plutus on the brink of the Fourth Circle? Of a sudden Dante hears the sound of a horn, so loud as to make the mightiest thunder weak.

CHAPTER THIRTEEN
THE TOWER OF HUNGER

Seeing not one but many lofty towers, dim in the distance, "Master," asks Dante, "what city is that?" Virgil takes him by the hand and tells him that those are not towers but Giants.

When the black mist fades, and the immensity of the Central Pit of Hell appears in all its fright, Dante sees six Giants around it with half their bodies showing. They are NIMROD, EPHIALTES, BRIAREUS, TITYOS, TYPHON, and ANTAEUS.

Nimrod, builder of the Tower of Babel and responsible for the confusion of languages, blows incoherent words into his horn: "Rafael Mai Amech Zabi Almi." His face is thirteen feet long, and swollen; his belly wide and only partly visible; and his arms hang immobile along his sides.

Ephialtes and Briareus, who once warred against high Jove, are not far away from Nimrod. Each shows an arm pinned behind his back, and the other immobilized on his chest by a huge chain that, coming down from the neck, goes five times about him before reaching the buried part of the body. But despite the hugeness of his chain, Ephialtes succeeds in shaking himself in anger, and such is the thunder that seems to threaten the whole pit that Dante fears for his life more than ever before.

It is to Antaeus, unchained, that Virgil speaks at this moment: "This man can give of that which here one longs for." Dante understands the meaning of these new words, not too dissimilar from the old password, "It is willed there, where what is willed is done." Upon hearing that Dante will mend his fame on earth, Antaeus does at once as he is told. He stretches forth his hands, and holds Virgil on them. Virgil, in turn, holds Dante tight in his arms, and thus the two are gently placed by the Giant on the bottom of Hell— a wide frozen lake called COCYTUS.

In this last Circle are punished the TRAITORS, those who denied, and froze, by their actions, the warmth of every natural tie. Even Treacherous Fraud is punished according to the law of retribution. These sinners are now held together by relentless ice, each holding his face bent toward the frozen surface of the lake, and each showing in his mouth and eyes the terror of his torture.

The NINTH CIRCLE is made of four concentric Rings. In the First, named CAINA after Cain who betrayed and slew his brother Abel, are the TRAITORS TO THEIR KIN. In the Second, named ANTENORA after Antenor, the Trojan who betrayed his City to the Greeks, are punished the TRAITORS TO THEIR COUNTRY. In the Third Ring... but wait: there is something here in

55

Antenora which sends an icy shudder through Dante's spine.

He is walking toward the middle of the Second Ring among a thousand faces violently disfigured by frostbite when, whether by chance or fate, he strikes with his foot one of those heads. "Why do you kick me?" cries that soul, in anguish. "Why do you want to hurt me, unless you come to take further vengeance for what I did at Montaperti?"

At this name Dante the Guelph recalls his meeting with Farinata the Ghibelline, and his blood beats fast in his heart. He knows quite well now that the fiery General is blamed on earth for all that bloodshed more than he should really be, and that someone else deserves perhaps much greater infamy among the Florentines.

"Who are you?" he asks the traitor he has inadvertently kicked.

"Who are *you*," answers the sinner scornfully, "who are passing through the Antenora, kicking other people's cheeks, which you could not do better if you were alive?"

"I *am* alive," replies Dante, "and can clear your name if you care to be remembered on earth."

"It's quite the opposite I want. Get out, and do not bother me any more."

"Either you tell me your name," shouts Dante, grabbing him by the hair with sudden anger, "or you won't have a hair left on this skull of yours."

"No," insists the anonymous traitor, "even if you pull my hair off not once but a thousand times, I will not tell you who I am.

Furiously Dante plucks out the first tuft of the sinner's hair when someone else's voice cries out: "What's wrong, Bocca? Is it not enough for you to chatter with your jaws? Must you bark too?"

"Ah, now that I know who you are," says Dante, "say not one word more, BOCCA DEGLI ABBATI, wicked traitor, for I will tell the truth about you.

"Go away," answers Bocca, "and say anything you please about me."

Virgil and Dante walk away only to see, not far from the treacherous Guelph, two other sinners, frozen in one hole, and one on top of the other. Dante gets closer to them and is faced with the most brutal and bestial scene imaginable: the one sinner is hungrily plunging his teeth into the other's nape, as if it were bread. Who are they, and what is the meaning of this horrid meal?

Asked to tell his story, the hungry traitor wipes first his mouth on the hair of the head whose nape he had already destroyed with his teeth, then says: "You ask me to relive a story of grief so desperate that the very thought of it wrings my heart before I even tell it to you. But if my words are to be a seed of infamy for the traitor I am gnawing, then I will speak in spite of all my tears. I do not know who you are nor how you could come down here, but, judging by your accent, I think you are from Florence. I am Count Ugolino and this is

Archbishop Ruggieri." Is there any Florentine who has not heard of COUNT UGOLINO and ARCHBISHOP RUGGIERI? The tragic story of the Pisan Count had shocked the world in 1289, only eleven years prior to Dante's journey through Hell. There were conflicting rumors about that story. Some people said that Count Ugolino had truly betrayed the City of Pisa by surrendering certain castles and fortresses to the Florentines and the Lucchese. Others believed that the real culprit was Archbishop Ruggieri, who first plotted with the Count and then had him arrested and imprisoned in the Tower together with four of his sons and grandsons. But what shocked the world was not whether the Count was less or more guilty than the Archbishop, but that the Count with his sons and grandsons had been left to starve to death. There was even the sordid rumor that hunger had made a cannibal of Ugolino.

Looking at the Count now weeping in front of him, his hands still savagely seizing the Archbishop's skull, and blood still dripping from the two corners of his unsated mouth, Dante thinks: "But how is it possible for a father to forget his tenderest feelings of love and affection, and feed on the dead flesh of his own children and grandchildren? No, it cannot be." But let the Count himself speak:

"I shall not tell you what you must have heard—
how I was taken and then put to death
for having trusted this man's wicked word.

"But I will tell you what no man can know—
how cruel was my death— and you will judge
if I was hurt, or not, by this my foe.

"A narrow opening above the prison,
now called the Tower of Hunger after me,
and which should punish other people's treason,

"had through its space already shown to me
several moons until a horrid dream
told me the future that was soon to be.

"A ruthless lord — in him this man I knew—
was chasing wolf and whelps up to the mount
that severs Lucca from the Pisans' view .

"After a while, father and children seemed

57

weary to me, but soon I saw lean hounds
rend them to pieces: this is what I dreamed.

"When I awoke before the dawn was shed,
I heard my children, who were there with me,
weep in their sleep and crave a bit of bread.

"You're made of stone if you grieve not, nor sigh,
thinking of what was certain in my heart:
if this does not, what then can make you cry?

"They too awoke, and now the hour drew near
    when food used to be brought; but each of them
because of the same dream was full of fear.

"And then the gate of that fierce tower I heard
being locked, below, forever: so I stared
at my sons' faces, uttering no word.
"I did not weep, for I within was stone.
They wept; and, 'Are you ill, who look at us
like that?' said Anselm, my dear little one.

"That's why I did not weep nor answer, all
    that day, nor the next night, until the sun
        rose on the world anew.

"As soon as a small ray peeped through the slit
    of that horrendous jail, and I could see
in their four faces my own face, I bit
"out of despair and grief on each my hand,
but thinking I had done it from desire
of food, all of them rose together and,

'Father,' they said, 'it gives us much less pain
if you will eat of us: this mortal flesh
    you gave us and is yours to take again.'

"I calmed myself then, not to grieve them more.
That day and the next day we all sat still.
Hard earth, why didn't you open then your floor?

"When to the dawn we came of the fourth day,
my Gaddo threw himself stretched at my feet,
and 'Why don't you help me, Father,~' I heard him say.

"And there he died; and as you now see me,
between the fifth and the sixth day I saw
fall one by one and die the other three.

"And it was then I groped in blindness, two
more days, on each dead body, calling them:
till fasting did what grief had failed to do."

Count Ugolino and Archbishop Ruggeri.

Ugolino's story is over. Dante sees him sink his teeth, as sharp as a dog's, into Ruggieri's skull once more, and thus resume his horrid meal. It is not important at this moment to know whether the Count's last line ("Till fasting did what grief had failed to do") means that he died of hunger, and not of grief, or whether it implies that hunger made him forget his grief.

The tragedy is in the fact that there will never be an answer to the question, and that Ugolino's last words will haunt our minds forever.

Cursing the entire City of Pisa for her cruelty to Ugolino's innocent sons and grandsons, Dante and Virgil leave the Antenora and move on to the Third Ring of the Ninth Circle, called PTOLOMEA after Ptolomaeus, the Biblical captain who invited his father-in-law Simon to his house where he treacherously killed him. In this part of the frozen, glassy lake are punished the TRAITORS TO THEIR FRIENDS AND GUESTS.

But something is new — look!

CHAPTER FOURTEEN
THE THREE MOUTHS AND SIX WINGS

The Traitors to Friends and Guests are not bent over like the previous traitors, but lie on their backs deep in the ice with only part of their faces showing above the frozen surface. They weep and at the same time are not allowed to weep. Finding impediment upon their eyes, their grief flows back into their hearts, and the first tears they shed form a knot of ice and, like crystal visors, fill up the eye-sockets.

Though the intense cold has made Dante's face numb, he feels a strange wind blowing all of a sudden. "Master," he asks Virgil, "who makes this wind blow?" "Soon you will see with your own eyes," replies Virgil. But before Dante reaches the presence of SATAN himself, he has to see what is really new and frightening about the Ptolomea —something that can happen only in this part of Hell.

Listen! "O souls, so cruel that you deserved this last Circle, remove the ice that has caked on my face, so that I may a bit relieve the grief that overfloods my heart before my weeping freezes again." The voice has come from one of the souls beneath the frozen surface of the lake.

"I will do as you say," says Dante to the sinner, "if first you tell me who you are."

"I am FRIAR ALBERIGO," answers the traitor who, one day on earth, invited his brother Manfred to a banquet and, at a signal ("Now serve the fruit") had him murdered. "I am the one of the wicked fruit."

"But you are not dead yet," says Dante, baffled.

"How my body is still in the world I do not know," explains Friar Alberigo, "but this is the privilege of the Ptolomea: many times a soul falls down here while its body is still alive. And so that you may more willingly scrape this glaze of tears off my face, I will tell you more. When the soul has done its treacherous deed, its body becomes the possession of a devil who rules it until the day of its death . . . That man down there, for instance, is BRANCA D'ORIA, and he has been here several years already."

"I believe you are lying to me," says Dante, "for Branca D'Oria is still very much alive, and eats and drinks and sleeps and changes clothes."

"Yes," explains Friar Alberigo with infernal joy in his voice, "but on the very day the man he had murdered fell into the Boiling Pitch, his soul came here, and his body on earth is still in the hands of a devil. Come now, reach out your hand and open my eyes."

But Dante does not dare interfere with God's justice, and, leaving the living traitor in his bed of ice, moves on behind Virgil to the very last depth of Hell.

The Fourth Ring of the Ninth Circle is called JUDECCA after Judas Iscariot, the apostle who betrayed Christ. Here are punished, frozen like shreds of straw in glass, the TRAITORS TO THEIR LORDS AND BENEFACTORS. Dante perhaps would like to recognize some of them but it is impossible to identify the twisted shadows imprisoned through the ice. Some are seen to be lying down; others appear to be standing either on their feet or on their heads; and others are so distorted as to make bows of their backs totally bent toward their feet.

When Dante sees something looking like a strange, huge building at the very center of Judecca, he knows that perhaps the worst moment of his journey has come, and draws close to Virgil, his only refuge now as ever. "Here is DIS," says his Master to him, "and now you must be strong." The word Dis is something which Dante would gladly forget. It reminds him of a thousand menacing ghosts above the gates of a weird city, and of three horrid serpent-haired Furies. But now that he knows who Dis is, he feels neither dead nor alive but a fossil himself like all the fossils around him. Does he at this moment think of the Heavenly Messenger who came to his rescue once before by opening the gate of the City of Dis with his magic wand? He only sees Lucifer, Lucifer himself, the Archtraitor, in front of him.

The one who wanted to be like the Unity and Trinity of God is now indeed a monstrous unity and trinity himself — one in three, and three in one. So much bigger than the biggest giants as to make any man seem one of them, Lucifer is now as ugly as he once was beautiful. He has three faces, each of a different color. The one in front is fiery red; and the other two are, one, between white and yellow, and the other, black.

Do you remember the words carved on the Gate of Hell, "I was created by Divine Omnipotence, Deep Wisdom, and First Love"? Satan is the opposite of all this—an appalling parody of Godhead. He is Impotence, Ignorance, and Hatred.

But what did Virgil mean by telling Dante to be strong? Is it possible that all this ice may suddenly thaw and bury the two visitors in its depth? Or is Satan, being Satan, going to show them the one thing he is allowed to do in his impotence, ignorance, and hatred? And how— how are they going to get out?

Dante takes a second terrified look at Satan. Under each of his three faces two enormous wings can be seen, all unfeathered and resembling in texture those of a bat. Every time he flaps them, three winds come forth from them—from him, rather— who, by doing this, keeps Cocytus frozen. A wing that cannot fly is a dead weight: Satan, therefore, is chained to his own wings and can only weep with his six eyes while his tears, mixed with bloody foam, trickle down not one but three chins.

But what is Satan doing with his three mouths? In each he rips a sinner with his teeth. In the one in front he tears to shreds JUDAS ISCARIOT, whose back, completely stripped of its skin, can at times be seen from below. The betrayer of Christ helplessly kicks his legs outside the chewing mouth, his head utterly buried in it. In the mouths on either side Satan executes BRUTUS and CASSIUS, the betrayers of Caesar. Fiercely they writhe and dangle from the cruel jaws, their heads out and over the last abyss of ice.

"Now clasp my neck tight," says Virgil to Dante, "for it is time to go." Saying no word, and happy to leave but terrified by the thought of the next moment of his journey, Dante clings to Virgil's neck with the strength of his last and worst terror.

With Dante holding on to him, Virgil takes advantage of the instant when Satan's wings are fully spread, and, seizing the shaggy sides of the Demon, from tuft to tuft slides down his tangled hair and frozen crusts until he reaches the place where the thigh turns into the swelling of the haunch. There with great difficulty and sweating, he turns upside down, placing his head where his feet had been, and only then grabs Satan's hair like one who is climbing, and not descending any more. Dante is frantic: are they going back toward Hell? "Hold fast!" says Virgil. "There is no other way for us but by such stairs to depart from all this evil."

At last, Virgil comes out of the Infernal Valley through the opening of a rock on whose edge he seats Dante before reaching it himself. Dante looks up and sees Lucifer as he had left him, but with his legs turned upward. "Up! Up on your feet!" says the Master. "The way is long, and savage is the road; and it is already half-past seven in the morning."

"Master," asks Dante, who can hardly believe his own eyes, "where is the ice? Why is he upside down? And why has the sun passed so quickly from night to morning?"

"You think you are still on the other side of the center where I grabbed the hair of the Evil Worm. You were on that side while I came down; but when I turned on myself you passed the center of gravity; so you are now under the Southern Hemisphere, with your feet upon the other face of Judecca. When it is evening there it's morning here. On this side Satan fell down from Heaven, and, in fear of him, the land that first was here rushed to our hemisphere, leaving this empty space behind."

Dante listens to Virgil's reply and yet his mind is deep in other thoughts. As in a flash he sees the three Wild Beasts, the Gate of Hell, the Boat of Charon, the Tombs on Fire, the Boiling Pitch, the Haunted Forest, the Lake of Ice, and Satan again. And faces, faces, new faces of sinners, all tormented, all doomed forever, seem to haunt him either to say farewell or to curse him or even to tell him they will be waiting for him. One thing seems clear to him now—how man's evil is punished by God's eternal Justice in innumerable ways.

The way is long, and savage is the road.

From the center of the earth Virgil and Dante now walk and walk through a narrow dark funnel alongside a little stream which is heard more than seen. A glimpse of the distant daylight leaks now and then through the crags overhead, telling them that Hell is at last behind them.

They do not stop until they reach the edge of the bright world and see the Stars once more.

Lucifer.

Purgatory

CHAPTER ONE
THE OLD MAN ON THE SHORE

It is Easter Sunday. Resurrection is in the air—a resurrection of bright colors in the sky, and of hope in Dante's heart.

How far behind is Hell? How far behind, Satan towering above the surface of the frozen lake?

Dante's misery belongs to the past now that his eyes, forced for one full day to look on nothing but darkness, can once again perceive the morning light blooming tenderly on the horizon.

How beautiful is Venus, the planet that heartens men to love! The eastern part of the sky is all one smile. But at this moment four other stars capture Dante's attention, so unusually bright they shine. Their blazing beauty seems to burn the earth and adorn the brow of a mysterious old man, motionless in front of Virgil and Dante.

Who can this old man be in this uninhabited corner of the universe, at the foot of a Mountain looming in the early shimmer of the day? Were it not for the rays of the four stars encircling his forehead like a halo, he would perhaps make Dante turn to his guide in fear. But Dante, instead, feels as if in the presence of a beloved father worthy of reverence.

But who is the old man? His beard is long and white, and his hair, equally dazzling, falls in two long, flowing tresses over his chest. Is all this light on his face the sun itself?

Filled with joyous astonishment, Dante is perhaps not even aware of the conversation between the old man, who is CATO OF UTICA, and Virgil.

"Who are you," says Cato, "who have just escaped from the eternal prison of Hell? Who brought you here out of the Everlasting Night? Are the laws of the Abyss suddenly broken?"

"Kneel down! Kneel down!" Virgil whispers to Dante, trying to make him understand the solemnity of the moment. Dante kneels and, still astonished, hears Virgil say to the Old Man:

"A Heavenly Lady sent me to this man's rescue. He has not seen the last of his evenings yet, but his foolishness brought him so close to it that he was almost part of its darkness. There was no other way to save him—believe me. I have already shown him the wicked spirits, and it is now my desire to show him the souls that cleanse themselves of all their sins. Oh, it would take too long to tell you how I brought him to your presence. God's grace has helped me in my task. It is freedom this man is seeking—a thing so dear that only those who die for it can appreciate it. You do, who for its sake found death a sweet experience. . . . No, we have not broken the laws of the Abyss, nor did Minos bind me with his tail. I come from Limbo. Please, let us go through your seven kingdoms...."

"If," Cato answers, smiling, "a Heavenly Lady, as you say, moves and directs you, you need but ask me in her name. Go then; but there are two things you must do for this man: first, bind a thin green reed around his waist, and then wash his face until the least stain is wiped away. He will soon meet an angel from Paradise, whom no one should dare approach with eyes still clouded by infernal mist. The thin green reed you will find down there at the extreme edge of this little island where the waves beat the shore. No other plant can bloom there. And one more thing: when you have done all this, do not come back this way. The rising sun will tell you how to reach the Mountain."

When Dante gets up, Cato is no longer in front of Virgil.

"Come, my son."

Uttering no word, Dante follows his teacher and lord.

Chased by the light of dawn, the morning air touches the sea and makes it tremble with myriad silvery bubbles, and the rising sun fights the last drops of dew, destroying them, all but a few, which still lie hidden in a shady corner.

Virgil stops right there, gathers those last few drops of dew, and washes Dante's face, removing from it the last remnants of the darkness of Hell. Then, at the extreme edge of the little island, where the waves beat the shore, Virgil plucks one of the thin green reeds and binds it around Dante's waist.

Dante has seen and suffered too much not to understand that this reed symbolizes humility. He knows that being human and frail he, too, has sinned like the souls punished in Hell, and must now learn in humility how to cleanse himself of his sins.

The sun, the shining grace of God, will tell him what to do.

But, look! A strange light is glimmering on the sea, and it seems to grow bigger and bigger, brighter and brighter. Something is coming ashore, faster than the fastest bird that ever flew.

CHAPTER TWO
A LOVE SONG

Does Virgil know what is happening? Dante turns to him to inquire, but as he receives no answer from his teacher he looks again at the mysterious light. He sees quite clearly now that something else is attached to that light—a white ornament on each side, and one, also white, beneath it. The approaching light is seen to take the shape of a boat with an Angel standing astern, his dazzling wings outspread toward heaven. The HEAVENLY PILOT needs no oars nor anything except his own bright wings to bring his ship to such a distant shore, and the ship itself is so swift and light that it hardly touches the water.

The Angel Pilot Bringing the Souls to Purgatory.

Dazzled by the new splendor, Dante lowers his glance. When he looks up again, he sees and hears that which he has never seen and heard before. He sees the Angel's face as a mirror of blessedness, and hears a magnificent chorus of a hundred voices in which sadness and joy are sweetly blended. But who is singing?

From the banks of the Tiber, the Heavenly Pilot has just brought more than a hundred souls to the foot of the Mountain of Purgatory. Now one by one they all come ashore while the Angel looks at them from the height of his vessel, smiling.

Dante can hear distinctly the words of the song the souls are singing, *In exitu Israel de Aegypto*. It is the psalm that tells of the deliverance of the children of Israel from their Egyptian captivity. How appropriate the song! Having died in God's grace, these new souls have just arrived from the captivity of both the earth and the body to the light of their eternal freedom. Their Egypt is over, then. Now it is only a question of time before they come to the vision of their Promised Land — Paradise.

Virgil and Dante listen intently to their sweet and sad choral music, so different from the horrible lamentations of the sinners in Hell.

When the singing of the psalm comes to an end, all the souls kneel down on the sand for the Angel's blessing. The Heavenly Pilot, standing on the stern of his ship, makes the sign of the Cross over them, and then sails away with the same speed with which Dante has seen him arrive.

The Mountain is fully visible in the light of the risen sun, but it is not easy to tell which way it can best be climbed. That is why all those souls, coming toward Virgil and Dante with a puzzled expression on their faces, decide to ask them about it. Our two poets, of course, do not know. They only remember the Old Man's words, that the sun will show them the way to the Mountain.

But now something totally unexpected happens. The souls realize that Dante is breathing. How can that be? Is he alive then? And if so, why is he among them? They are not frightened, for only sin should frighten one and, being saved, they can no longer offend their God. They are only amazed at what they see.

It is their amazement that makes them gather around the living man as people on earth do when, eager for news of home, they surround the one who has just arrived from their native town. Oh, if this man is still alive, it can only mean that he is fresh from the earth, their earth, and surely has happy tidings to relate. But why are they so eager to know about a world they have hardly left? Do they still believe that death has not destroyed their feelings of affection and love? Earth, sweet earth!

One of the souls recognizes Dante and with great cordiality moves forward to embrace him. Dante wants to do the same but, to his great embarrassment, his arms three times fall back onto his own chest. Not unlike those he has seen in Hell, these souls look indeed like real persons, but they are only shadows— and can you ever embrace a shadow?

CASELLA, the first Florentine friend Dante meets in Purgatory, on earth was a skillful musician, and also endowed with a pleasant singing voice. He had set to music some of Dante's love poems, which he used to sing at joyous gatherings.

"My dear Casella," says Dante, his heart overcome with nostalgia, "if you still remember that song of love which used to satisfy my every wish, and if your new condition does not forbid you to sing, comfort a bit my soul which, coming here together with its body, is weary, oh, so weary!"

In one of his poems Horace says that poets, like singers, love to be coaxed, but once they start they are not willing to stop. Not so Casella.

As soon as he hears that his friend is weary and needs comfort, he begins to sing. His impulse is motivated by charity, and charity has no time to inquire about old or new regulations. And what does he sing? A song of human, earthly love in a realm where only love of God should be the aspiration of every soul.

"Love that within my mind is reasoning."

Casella keeps singing, and the music of the old song sounds so new that not only Dante but even Virgil and all the souls listen to the rapture of its notes, unaware, it seems, of all other things. It is a moment of beauty in which past, present, and future seem to meet. But has Dante forgotten that earthly beauty is only a pale glimpse, or a faint echo, of God's imperishable beauty? And Virgil, who should know better, has he forgotten that it is his duty to make Dante understand that the sooner he gets home, that is, to the beauty and warmth of God's grace, the better it is for his soul?

No one seems to remember that the Mountain is waiting in the sheen of the new day.

But there is one who knows the meaning of freedom too well to put up with this childish play.

"What is this?" shouts Cato, appearing suddenly in the midst of the group, and interrupting their song. "Have you forgotten why you are here? Run to the Mountain, and start your cleansing, or you will never be able to see God."

Just as a flock of pigeons, disturbed at the best moment of their meal, scatter in every direction, so at these words do all the souls flee in mortified silence toward the Mountain.

Feeling responsible for what has just happened, Virgil, too, hurries in the same direction with Dante following close behind.

CHAPTER THREE
A KING BURIED AND UNBURIED

Dante is suddenly afraid. The sun, flaming red behind him, casts his shadow directly in front of him. Is he alone? Has his beloved guide abandoned him?

Virgil reassures him by telling him that it is now evening in the place where his body, which used to cast a similar shadow, lies buried. He should not be afraid but have faith, instead. Is he perhaps marveling at the fact that the heavenly spheres can shine without obstructing each other's light? There are so many things the human mind will never be able to fathom! How much better it is, then, simply to believe.

Finally, the two reach the foot of the Mountain, where the rock is too steep for even the most agile athlete to climb. One needs wings for this uncommon task, and Dante, unfortunately, is still imprisoned in the heaviness of his body. If only there were someone to tell them what to do!

It is Dante who sees a throng of souls coming slowly around the Mountain, so slowly that they seem not to be moving at all.

"Master," he says, "there, look there! People are coming who may tell us what to do." But so slowly are the souls advancing that, not to waste time, Virgil and Dante decide to walk toward them.

After about a thousand paces they are as far as a good sling shot away from the throng when all those souls, stopping in sudden amazement, huddle against the hard rocks of the cliff, staring, motionless, at Dante. Only when Virgil begs them to tell him how to reach a slope easy to climb does the chief of those souls seem to move forward, in deep astonishment.

As sheep come out through the gate of a pen by ones, by twos, by threes, and all the others follow, eyes and nose to the ground, and what the first does the others do, silent and meek, stopping if the first one stops: so are these new souls moving forward toward Dante and Virgil. (They are the EXCOMMUNICATED, those who were excommunicated by the Church but died in God's grace by repenting of their sins at the moment of death.) They all step backward when the first of them steps backward, wondering, on noticing Dante's shadow.

Virgil explains to them that the man whose shadow goes from him to the rock is truly alive, but he adds that it was through heavenly power that he was allowed to come to the Mountain.

"Very well then," say all the souls, pointing to one particular slope, "you go ahead. We will come right behind you.

But, one of the Late-Repentant spirits—a blond-haired, handsome youth with a regal air about him—asks if Dante ever saw him on earth. No, Dante believes he never did, and so he apologizes for not recognizing the youth.

Once more, as in the case of Casella, it seems that the earth, with all its little incidents of pride or affection, is present in this realm of the spirit.

Proudly now, as though he were still on earth, the young man shows his two wounds to the unusual visitor from the world of the living. By those two wounds—one on the eye and the other above his chest—he thinks that Dante should recognize him, for everybody knows how bravely he fought and met death on the battlefield. But before Dante apologizes again, the young man smiles, realizing how futile it is, at the foot of the Mountain of Purgatory, to remember an irrelevant episode ended in dust. "I am MANFRED," he says in all humility, and, thinking that his name alone may not be sufficient to disclose his full identity to Dante, he adds, "grandson to Empress Constance."

So this handsome youth is MANFRED, son of Frederick II, Emperor of the Two Sicilies. Dante was one year old when Manfred was defeated and killed at the Battle of Benevento, in 1266.

For the first time, a soul in Purgatory tells the story of his life and death.

Everybody on earth believes Manfred to be lost in Hell because of the excommunication inflicted upon him by Pope Clement IV. But here he is, instead, among the souls who will some day ascend to Heaven and be with God forever. What is the meaning of this? Does the word of a Pope mean nothing then, if though condemned by the authority of the Vicar of Christ and cut off from the Church, one can still go to Heaven?

When, at the Battle of Benevento, Manfred lay wounded on the ground, he turned to God — the One who willingly forgives. His sins had been horrible, but in His infinite mercy God welcomes all those who seek refuge in His arms. That was the last moment of Manfred's existence on earth but, also, the first of his true life with God.

His soldiers buried him under the safeguard of a heavy cairn on top of a bridge near Benevento. But when Pope Clement heard the happy news of Manfred's defeat and death, he ordered the Bishop of Cosenza to have the young king's body disinterred and laid on the banks of the Verde River, that is, outside the boundaries of the Church States. The body of one who was surely in Hell — thus thought the Pope — should not remain on blessed ground. The Bishop of Cosenza obeyed promptly.

The heavy cairn was beaten down stone by stone. Ropes were tied around the arms and feet of the frozen body, and at night, without candles, without prayers, as if it were the carcass of an animal, it was dragged for miles as far as the banks of the river, where it was left to the wrath of the wind and the rain.

"But let me tell you one thing," Manfred hastens to add. "It is not the curse of a Pope or a Bishop that seals the eternal punishment of a soul. While one is alive there is still hope, and while there is hope for repentance, it is God who says the last word. Has Pope Clement forgotten that God is not only Justice but also Mercy? If he had remembered that, my bones would still be under the heavy cairn at Benevento, whereas the rain now wets them and the winds toss them about."

Why does Manfred, who smiled a while ago in remembering an earthly detail of his life, now seem so hurt by the thought of the storm tossing his poor remains on the bank of a river? The thought of his eternal salvation should give him joy and make him forget all else.

But there is something Dante does not yet know. Though they repented at the moment of death and thus died within God's grace, contrary to the Pope's belief, these souls must wait here around the base of the Mountain for a period thirty times as long as that of their excommunication on earth, unless good prayers should shorten it. Only then will they begin their cleansing.

That is why Manfred ends his story with these words: "See if you can make me happy by revealing to my good daughter Constance that you saw me among the saved, and that the good prayers of the living can do so much for us in Purgatory."

CHAPTER FOUR
A DEVIL, AN ANGEL, AND A CORPSE

In the brightness of the morning another group of Late Repentants can be seen moving slowly at the base of the cliff: they are the INDOLENT, those who, whether murdered or killed on a battlefield, turned to God at the moment of death but had no time to confess their sins to a priest.

They are singing the Miserere, one of the Seven Penitential Psalms, over and over. On hearing that first word, Dante cannot but recall his own cry for help when Virgil appeared to him in the Dark Forest.

It is help these new souls are seeking — help from God in Heaven and from the living on earth. Only thus will the period of their futile waiting below the Mountain be shortened. But as soon as they, too, notice Dante's shadow on the ground, their choral singing turns suddenly into a prolonged "Oh" of wonder, which is so human and at the same time so dramatic.

A living man walking among them is not an ordinary event, and so they send two of their group as messengers to Virgil and Dante. They are eager to know whether what they have seen is not just a figment of their imagination.

"Tell all the souls that they are right in their belief. This man is indeed alive, and what you see is really his flesh. Tell them, also, that he can help them with his prayers."

The two messengers go back at once, and relate the happy news to the group.

Knowing that someone is there who can do so much for them, the souls run fast toward Dante, wishing to introduce themselves. But Virgil warns his pupil not to stop or they will never start climbing the Mountain. Dante must therefore keep walking while listening to them.

"I was known as Buonconte of Montefeltro, but am now simply Buonconte," says one of them. The greatest dejection imaginable seems to be written on his brow. "No one prays for me, no one, not even Giovanna, my wife. If you at least could help me!"

BUONCONTE OF MONTEFELTRO — how well Dante re- members that name! It reminds him of the Battle of Campaldino, in 1289, and that battle reminds him of something else— that he, too, had been a soldier and borne arms in defense of his beloved Florence. All of a sudden he recalls every detail of that victory over the rebellious Ghibellines of Arezzo, and, above all, the mysterious disappearance of Buonconte, the defeated General. At the end of the battle, Dante had joined the other Florentine warriors in the search for him. They knew he had been wounded, and had been seen running toward the Archiano River, leaving a trail of blood on the plain. Wounded and bleeding as he was, he could not have walked far. He had to be somewhere, dead or dying behind a rock, or under a bush or a tree.

No, he could not have walked far. They kept searching for him throughout the night, and what a night that was. Never before had they seen such a storm. The sky seemed to fall headlong upon the earth with an infernal fury of thunderbolts, and the earth seemed not to exist any more, such was the rain that was covering it, mercilessly, timelessly drowning everything on it. But still the Florentine soldiers kept looking for Buonconte. When the sun rose the following morning, they were exhausted. The rain had wiped away every drop of blood, and, except for a few corpses half-visible in the mud, there was hardly a vestige of the battle of the day before. Another look around served no purpose at all: Buonconte's body could not be found. The victorious Florentine soldiers went home without their most precious trophy, but for a long time they kept wondering about Buonconte's baffling end.

Eleven years have elapsed but the remembrance of that battle and of that search is still alive in Dante's mind. But here is the General now, right before one of those soldiers.

"What happened to your body?" Dante asks, as though nothing else mattered.

Buonconte smiles, and there is a mixture of sadness and joy in his smile. Were it not for the happy recollection of his salvation attached to the story of his death, he would perhaps not understand the human curiosity behind Dante's question. But to tell about his body means to talk about his soul, for it is exactly because of his soul that his body disappeared in a way that no man on earth can ever suspect.

"Pierced in the throat," he answers, "and bloodying the plain behind me, I reached the place where the Archiano enters the Arno River and thus loses its identity. There I lost vision, there the last word I said was 'Mary!' and there my spirit left my flesh.

"What I am about to tell you is the truth, and see to it that men on earth know it also.

"An Angel from Heaven took my soul, and a devil from Hell shouted: 'O you from Heaven, why do you rob me? For one little word, for one little tear that snatches him from me, you are taking the better part of him. Very well, take his soul with you; but I will take his body, and do what I please with it.'

"At once he united evil will with evil intellect, and set in motion mist and wind by the power which his nature gave him.

"Then, when night came, he covered the valley with fog from Pratomagno to the Apennines, and made the sky above bend lower and lower until the saturated air turned into water. The rain fell, so much of it that what the earth could not receive flowed on along trenches and ditches in great torrents so sweeping and swift that nothing could tame them.

"The swollen Archiano found my frozen body at its mouth, swept it into the Arno, and loosed on my breast the cross which I had made of my arms when sorrow for my sins overcame me. Along its banks and over its bed the Arno tossed and turned me until it wrapped and buried me under its debris."

Dante is given no time to promise Buonconte that he will relate his story among the living, for another soul is eager to be heard—PIA DE' TOLOMEI.

It is the soft, gentle voice of a woman that comes to relieve the tension in Dante's spirit.

"When you return to the world, and are well rested from your long journey, may you then remember me. My name is Pia."

What tenderness in these words! Never before has Dante heard so kind an expression of concern about his well-being.

True, even in hell, many souls had asked to be remembered among the living, but not one of them had ever thought of Dante's need for rest after his long and wearisome journey among the dead.

Pia has little to say. All she wishes to remember of her life on earth is that she was born in Siena and unjustly killed in the swampy region of the Maremma. But, unlike Francesca da Rimini, she does not accuse her husband; instead she recalls something beautiful and tender—the moment, of her wedding day, when he made her his wife by placing a ring on her finger as if to tell Dante that her

Buonconte's body swept by the river.

76

beloved Nello should not be blamed for taking her life, but only judged by that troth of love and loyalty to her.

Is Dante thinking, at this moment, of his blessed Beatrice? She, too, did not want Virgil to know the tragic truth about a certain person lost in the Dark Forest when she referred to him as "my friend, and not a friend of fortune."

CHAPTER FIVE
THE SNAKE IN THE FLOWERS

Every Late-Repentant soul begs for prayers, and Dante, who cannot but listen to each of them, seems to forget that time is flying and the Mountain still far away. He does not know that he will have to spend the night outside the Gate of Purgatory.

But who will show the two pilgrims the easiest shortcut to the place of cleansing?

Finally, they see a soul sitting all alone, apart from all the others and in a seemingly disdainful mood. Who can it be? It does not matter. The only thing that counts is to know where to climb the Mountain.

It is Virgil who asks the question. But, instead of answering, that solitary spirit asks, in turn, another question: "Where are you from?"

"Mantua . . ." Virgil replies, but is given no time to add "is the town I come from." No longer disdainful but unexpectedly cheerful and happy, the soul leaps toward Virgil and embraces him, saying, "I am SORDELLO. I am from Mantua, too."

At the sight of such a joyful reunion, Dante thinks of the terrible political chaos in his own Italy. "Look at these two," he says to himself. "They embrace each other, they are happy simply because they come from the same town, whereas in this land of mine, city is against city, and family against family. Ah, why does God allow all this to happen?"

Sordello embraces fellow Mantuan Virgil.

When Sordello is told that the Mantuan he has embraced three and four times is none other than Virgil, he falls at his feet in amazement and admiration. But Virgil tells him to rise and asks him about the shortcut to the Mountain. Sordello offers to lead the two pilgrims and explains the law of the place to them. No soul can ascend the Mountain after the sun goes down, and even if one tried to climb during the night every attempt would be in vain: he would not be able to take one single step forward.

"There is a lovely valley down below," Sordello points out, "where nature displays all its beauty. There you may spend the night, talking to people you will be happy to meet."

So down to that valley go Virgil, Dante, and Sordello, while the notes of the *Salve Regina* tenderly fill the air.

Easter Sunday is coming to an end. The sun is dropping fast below the horizon.

It was the hour that makes man's fancy sway,
And melts the hearts of those who far at sea
Remember tender friends left on that day;

The hour that a new pilgrim instantly
Pierces with love if far away a bell
Is heard to mourn the day about to flee.

In the sweetness of this first sunset in the Underworld, and while all sounds are beginning to grow faint, Dante meets a new group of souls, with their glances lifted up to heaven. One of them intones the evening prayer that begins with the words *"Te lucis ante terminum,"* and all the others join in the singing to ask the Creator of all things to save them from the phantoms of the night.

The phantoms of the night? Is there danger, then, in Purgatory, when the sun goes down? Or is it only in this lovely valley that the night seems to be charged with sinister omens?

All these thoughts flash suddenly through Dante's mind, and to make them the more disquieting, something happens that he fails to understand.

At the end of the evening prayer the souls grow pale and visibly frightened. Uttering no sound, they all look up to heaven, their hands still joined and raised in mid-air.

A few unbearable moments elapse before two Angels come down from above for the protection of the valley. Their garments are of a tender green like newly sprouted leaves, and their wings, also green, seem to be fanning the length of their garments. So dazzling is the light on their faces that Dante cannot see their eyes. But he can see the beauty of their golden hair—and something else. Each of the two Angels wields a flaming sword, broken short and devoid of its point.

"They come from Mary's bosom," says Sordello, "to protect the valley from the snake that will come in a short while."

Frightened by these words, and not knowing from where the serpent will come, Dante draws closer to Virgil, who does not say a word to relieve his sudden fear.

A snake will come in a short while! It cannot be an ordinary snake if two Angels have been sent from Heaven to protect the whole valley. It must be the devil, if Mary herself, the Blessed Mother who first saw Dante's predicament in the Dark Forest, has decided to send not one but two of her Angels to save her children from temptation. But how can this be? There should not be any temptation here in Purgatory, for there cannot be any future sin among these souls.

Darkness is coming, but there is still a glimpse of light over the valley, so Dante can see a few souls quite near him. In fact, he even recognizes one of them—JUDGE NINO VISCONTI OF GALLURA.

How good it is at a moment of danger to meet somebody you know!

The two old friends greet each other as warmly as they used to do on earth.

"How long is it since you came to the foot of the Mountain?" asks Nino, believing Dante to be dead.

"I arrived this morning from the place of evil," replies Dante, "and am still in my first life."

At these words Sordello turns to Virgil, and Judge Nino to another soul sitting not far away from him, saying, "Come, Conrad, come! Come to see what God has willed by His grace!"

"Oh, then," Judge Nino tells Dante in a different tone of voice, "when you go back to the world, tell my daughter Giovanna to pray for me. I don't think her mother loves me any more, since she has remarried. But it would have been much better for her to remain a widow . . . Well, one can see from her case how long the fire of love lasts in a woman if sight and touch do not rekindle it often."

Three bright stars can now be seen in the sky, just where the four stars had shone in the morning. Virgil is still telling Dante about them when, "See there our enemy," says Sordello, pointing his finger to something in the grass.

Amid the grass and flowers the evil snake is coming, turning its head now and again to its back, and licking like a beast that sleeks itself.

What will happen now?

The two Angels move so fast against the reptile that Dante does not see them until they are already charging. Hearing the green wings cleaving the

The snake in the flowers.

darkened air, the serpent flees in defeat. The Angels return to their posts for the rest of the night.

Only now can Dante understand the meaning of what has happened. The appearance of the evil snake serves only one purpose—to remind the souls of the dreadful danger of sin from which God has forever delivered them. It is like a nightmare at the end of which the souls in the valley can appreciate more keenly the grace of their eternal salvation.

But CONRAD MALASPINA, the one called by Judge Nino at the sudden discovery of Dante's being alive, has not paid any attention, it seems, to what has just taken place in the valley. He has been staring and staring at the singular visitor.

"If you have news of Valdimacra, my land," he says, introducing himself, "tell me about it."

"Oh," answers Dante, "I have never been there, but is there anybody in Europe who has not heard of the valor and generosity of your house, the only one that scorns the crooked paths of the world?"

"Very well," says Conrad, "but in less than seven years, if what has been decreed is not altered, you will know the generosity of my family not by hearsay but through personal experience."

In other words, in less than seven years Dante will be in Valdimacra and in need of a piece of bread. What a sad prophecy!

And so the first day in Purgatory comes to an end, but what a long day it has been! And in a few hours Dante and Virgil will face the Angel Doorman. Will he let a living man pass through the mighty door?

Feeling the burden of time, Dante falls asleep.

CHAPTER SIX
SEVEN P'S ON DANTE'S FOREHEAD

At daybreak, Dante dreams that an eagle has snatched him away from his bed and carried him up to the Gate of Purgatory. When he awakens, he is told by Virgil that his dream was no dream at all. At the end of the night Saint Lucy had come from Heaven and carried him, in his sleep, up the difficult slope of the Mountain to the threshold of the mighty door.

It is Easter Monday, and the new sun shines beautiful and bright, casting its rays on the Gate of Purgatory.

Dante looks about, half-sleepy, half-dazed, like one who, awakening in a strange, unfamiliar place, wonders how he got there.

But there is the Gate, shining and still locked. Three steps, each of a different color, lead to it, and on the third stands an Angel, silent and with a sword in his hand.

Finally, Virgil and Dante hear these words: "Answer from where you are: What are you seeking, and who brought you here? See that your climbing brings you no harm!"

Once again, as he did in the presence of Cato, Virgil speaks out for Dante. "A Lady from Heaven," he replies, "told us a while ago: 'The Gate is there; go ahead!'"

"Very well," says the ANGEL OF THE CHURCH, "and may she guide your journey on to a fruitful end! Come forward then!"

All of a sudden, Dante realizes the moment has come for him to confess his sins. He who has seen how sin is punished in Hell feels now compelled to admit his own guilt.

Upon setting foot on the first of the three steps, which is made of bright, white marble, he can see himself as he really is. He sees his own conscience reflected in that piece of marble as clearly, it seems, as only God could see it.

The second step is made of a rough, burnished stone, cracked both lengthwise and across and its color is bluish-black. Immediately, Dante feels sorryabout his sins. It is as though his heart, too, were cracking at the thought of One who had died on the Cross for him.

The third and final step is so flaming red it seems to be made of porphyry. All of a sudden, Dante understands that to confess and feel sorry about his sins is not enough. He has to do penance, even if it means that his heart must bleed.

The threshold of the door upon which the Angel stands seems to be adamantine stone, and, instantly, Dante understands the meaning of it. It reminds him of the solid rock upon which Christ founded His Church—a rock that not even the fury of Hell can shake.

At this point, Dante does not know what to do, but Virgil promptly tells him to kneel at the Angel's feet and humbly ask his forgiveness.

Our pilgrim falls to his knees and begs for mercy, beating his breast three times. The Angel carves with the point of his sword seven *P*'s on Dante's forehead, saying, "See that you wash these wounds when you are inside."

After what has happened, Dante knows full well what these seven P's mean. *P* being the first letter of the Latin word *peccatum*, which means "sin," they represent the Seven Capital Sins. From now on, as he climbs from cornice to cornice, it will be his duty to remove these *P*'s from his forehead, one at a time, until he is all cleansed and ready for Heaven. One *P* would not be enough. Though his name is Dante, he symbolizes mankind and, being guilty of all sins, he must therefore pay for all of them.

But will the Angel show mercy? Will he now open the Gate of Purgatory?

From under his tunic—look—he draws out two keys, one of gold and one of silver. Finally he unlocks the Gate, using first the golden key and then the one of silver.

The Angel explains that, in giving him those keys, Saint Peter told him to use them as many times as people should fall at his feet, asking for mercy.

Dante feels absolved of all his sins as the massive Gate opens in front of him with a thundering sound of joy.

"Enter," the Angel says, "but let me warn you that he who looks behind finds himself outside again."

The sound made by the pivots of the sacred door is so loud that Dante can hardly hear the notes of the *Te Deum laudamus* coming from inside. All the souls in Purgatory are praising God, thanking Him for allowing another spirit to start its ascent and cleansing.

CHAPTER SEVEN
PERVERTED LOVE

THE PROUD are punished in the first of the Seven Cornices of the Mountain. But where are they?

Dante must not look back but only ahead, and there seems to be nothing ahead but the rough surface of the Mountain.

Finally, he notices that the inner side of that rugged wall is of pure white marble carved with scenes from the Old Testament and pagan history, so beautiful and artistically perfect that not only the great sculptor Polycletus but Nature herself would be unable to imitate. They are scenes that teach humility to one who looks at them.

In one, the Virgin Mary, so realistically carved that she seems alive, is seen in the act of saying *"Ecce Ancilla Dei"* to Gabriel, the Archangel of the Annunciation. In another Dante recognizes the Roman Emperor Trajan on his way to war. But who is the little old woman in the act of talking to him?

This is the story. One day, as Trajan was on his way to war, he was stopped by a poor widow in tears. He was surrounded by mounted officers and a multitude of banners on which the golden eagles seemed to flutter in the wind. But she had to see him, and so she managed to get near him. "My Lord," she said,

The Souls of the Proud.

"my son has been slain, and I want justice done." "Wait till I come back," replied the Emperor. "What if you do not?" the old lady asked promptly. And the Emperor: "The one who takes my place will do it." Whereupon the grief-stricken mother asked: "How can another person's good be your concern if you forget your own?" And, finally, the Emperor said to her: "Be assured. It is indeed my duty to act now, not when I return. Justice demands it; pity halts me here."

"Look to your left," Virgil says to Dante, removing him from the contemplation of those lovely scenes.

Dante sees, coming slowly

from the left side of the cornice, several human "forms" bent under heavy burdens of stone, so twisted and crumpled up that to look at them gives him an agonized sense of discomfort. And yet those forms have one desire—to lower themselves more and more under their crushing weight. As they come nearer, Dante hears a beautiful, tender song, the first hymn inside the Mountain of Purgatory. It sounds like the Lord's Prayer.

Our Father, who in all Thy heavens art,
Not circumscribed, but through the greater love
Thou hast for wonders that were first to start,

Praised be Thy name and Thy unending worth
By every creature, as indeed 'tis meet
That Thy sweet effluence be thanked on earth.

May Thine own Kingdom's peace to us arrive,
For we cannot to its first solace come,
However hard we think and hard we strive.

As of their will Thine angels make to Thee
Full sacrifice, Hosanna singing all,
So may men make of theirs in unity.

Our daily manna give to us this day,
Without which on this desert rough and harsh
He who most toils to go, goes most astray.
And as we now forgive each suffered ill,
Do Thou forgive in mercy and in love,
And regard not the merit of our will.

Put not our virtue, crumbling at each blow,
To trial with our ancient enemy,
But spare us from him who can prick it so.

Dante is recognized by one of the Proud—ODERISI OF GUBBIO, once a great illuminator of manuscripts on earth. How differently he talks now from the way he used to in his mortal days. He had deemed himself the greatest artist in the world, and now, bent beneath the massive stone that disfigures him, he is eager to have Dante know that human fame is nothing but a breath of wind capriciously blowing in this and that direction. A thousand years from now, what difference will there be between one who died an infant and one who died an old man? 0 empty glory of human power! How short a time a leaf stays green on the bough of a tree if a sudden storm does not come to make its life shorter still!

After these words, Oderisi of Gubbio points his finger at another proud man not far from him—PROVENZAN SALVANI, the one who once had Siena at his feet. Ah, he would not be here in Purgatory if at the end of his life he had not humbled himself for the sake of a friend—an act of humility and charity for which God forgave him his previous sin of pride aud welcomed him among the Elect.

In order to listen to Oderisi, Dante, too, has been walking along bent in humility, his own thoughts of pride utterly crushed and shrunken.

"Why don't you look down," says Virgil, "at the pavement of the rock? It will do you good."

Dante looks down at the pavement he is treading and to his amazement sees, limned along the floor, the figures of several haughty spirits ruined by pride — Satan, Briareus, Thymbraeus, Nimrod, Niobe, Saul, Arachne, Rehoboam, Eriphyle, Sennacherib, Cyrus, and Holofernes.

How clear everything is now! The proud are humbled and trampled on across the floor whereas the humble are exalted along the mountainside.

"All right, lift up your eyes now," says Virgil. "See there an Angel coming toward us. It is already past noon.

Dante lifts up his eyes and sees the new Angel coming toward them, bright and tremulous like the morning star.

The ANGEL OF HUMILITY, opening his arms and spreading his wings, points out to the two visitors the steps by which to climb to the second cornice and, as though his words were not enough, most graciously he leads them there himself. Then, with a stroke of his wing he touches Dante's forehead, and promises him a safe journey.

Virgil and Dante start climbing to their right when a new hymn, *Beati pauperes spiritu,* is suddenly heard in the air.

Dante feels happy and agile. Is it perhaps the new music that gives him such a wonderful feeling of spiritual and even physical relief?

When Virgil explains to him that the first of the seven *P*'s is no longer on his forehead, Dante brings the fingers of his right hand to it so as to count the remaining letters. Yes, there are six of them left.

Virgil smiles, amused.

THE ENVIOUS are punished in the Second Cornice, and what a punishment that is! They who on earth were blind to the good of their fellow mortals, and only wished them unhappiness, are now reminded of their sin of envy in a way that makes one shudder: their eyes are stitched up with wire.

Leaning against one another for support, they grope like blind beggars—they who once believed in nothing but their own success. Though the sun is still bright, there is no light for these souls. The stone they tread is gray, and gray the color of the sackcloth that they wear.

Walking among them seeing but not seen, Dante feels sorry for them, and would surely like to know if there are Italians in this cornice.

"O people assured of seeing the Light above," he says, when Virgil tells him to address the new throng, "is there any Italian among you?"

"Brother," a voice is heard from the group, "each of us is a citizen of the same true City; but perhaps you mean one who was once a pilgrim in Italy."

"O spirit," Dante says promptly, "if you are the one who has just answered me, please tell me where you come from and who you are."

"I come from Siena," the soul replies, "and, although my name was SAPIA, there was no 'sapience' in me. No, I am not deceiving you. How foolish I was, you can judge for yourself.

"When the arc of my years was declining, my townsmen met their foes near Colle, and oh, how I prayed for their defeat! Soon they were routed and bitterly chased by the victor, and seeing that chase, such joy I felt that I lifted up my defying glance, shouting to God: 'I fear You no more.'

"With God I made peace at the end of my life, and had it not been for Peter the Comb-seller, the holy man who in his charity prayed for me, I would not be here now.

"But who are *you*, who are inquiring about us and, as I believe, can see and breathe?"

'I won't be here long," replies Dante, "for the fear of the cornice below affects me more than I can tell."

"Who has brought you, then, up here among us," Sapia asks, "if you think you will go back again?"

"The one who is with me and says no word. I am not dead, and if, therefore, you want me to help you, you need but ask me."

"Oh, this is so new a thing that it only means God loves you; therefore remember me sometimes in your prayers. And, if ever you tread the Tuscan land again, restore my fame among my kinsfolk.

After Sapia, other souls introduce themselves to Dante while mysterious voices warning against envy ring in the air.

Finally, the ANGEL OF GENEROSITY removes another P from Dante's brow, and tells the two visitors that they have reached the stair leading to the next cornice. But where is all this fog coming from? It is suddenly dark.

THE WRATHFUL are punished in the Third Cornice, where Virgil and Dante see at once, as in an ecstatic vision, sublime examples of meekness and patience.

But in what way are these new souls cleansing themselves to be worthy of Christ, the meek Lamb of God? Their punishment is frightful. It consists of a smoke so thick, so dark that the very gloom of Hell is nothing in comparison. Think of the most horrid night, with not one star to be seen and with black, low clouds hovering over the earth, and you will have but a faint notion of the darkness that envelops the souls of the Wrathful.

One of them introduces himself as MARCO LOMBARDO, once a liberal, learned courtier.

It is he who, after assuring Dante that he and his guide are on the right path to the next ascent, also explains to our living pilgrim why the world is so blind and full of vice.

"The world," says Dante, "is devoid of every virtue and immersed in sin; but tell me why this has come to pass, so that, knowing the causes, I may point them out to others."

Marco heaves a sigh.

"Brother," he replies, "the world you come from is blind indeed. But you, who are still living, like to trace every cause back to the stars as if they were responsible for all the things that happen. If it were so, there would be no Free Will left in you. . . . Yes, it is from the stars that your instincts begin, but not

The Souls of the Gluttons.

all of them. And even if I said 'all,' a light is also given you that makes you see what is good and what is evil, and with it, Free Will, which, though at first it seems to struggle with God, ultimately conquers all, if properly handled.

"In your freedom, you can aspire to a greater power and to a better nature; and it is exactly this that makes your mind what it is—a thing the stars cannot control.

"Therefore, if today the world is wicked, it is you, and you alone, who are responsible for its wickedness."

Marco Lombardo says other pertinent things, and Dante listens to him with great attention.

The sun is setting now, and the second day in Purgatory is coming to its end. It is pitch-dark.

But suddenly the light of the ANGEL OF MEEKNESS, standing on the first step that leads to the Fourth Cornice, breaks the gloomy darkness with its flashing whiteness. Once again, Dante feels the stroke of the Angel's wing on his forehead, and so he knows that another *P* has been removed.

Thus ends the first part of Purgatory, in which man's perverted love is punished.

CHAPTER EIGHT
DEFECTIVE LOVE

In the Fourth Cornice are punished THE SLOTHFUL. They are those who in their existence on earth were not diligent enough to pursue the Good which they recognized. As they were sluggish and lazy then, so are they quick and overzealous now. They keep running and running within the boundaries of their Cornice as if nothing could stop them. The sloth of their ancient life has now become a powerful whip.

It is their noisy rush that, around midnight, awakens Dante from his first brief slumber. Still half-asleep, he sees the new souls moving rapidly by him, and understands that they cannot stop even to ask for prayers.

In the very front of the throng, two of them shout in tears:

"Mary ran in haste to the hill country" and "To subdue Ilerda, Caesar first tamed Marseilles and then rushed to Spain."

All the others understand the meaning of these two examples of spiritual and temporal zeal, and answer in unison:

"Hurry! Hurry! Let's waste no time through little love, so that each new effort may bring God's grace back to us."

"O souls," says Virgil, "whose fervor now makes up for your old negligence and delay in well-doing, this man—I am not lying to you—is alive, and eager to climb up as soon as the new sun appears. Tell us, therefore, where we can find the steps to the next cornice."

"Come right behind us," replies THE ABBOT OF SAN ZENO, one of the Slothful, "and you will find the opening.

We are so eager to keep moving that we cannot stop. Therefore forgive us if what is our penance seems rudeness to you."

When all the hasty souls are out of sight, new thoughts cross Dante's mind, and then others, and then others, until, completely lost in them, he falls sound asleep.

The moon looks like a burning bucket in the midst of other stars.

As the light of the third day approaches, Dante has a dream—the DREAM OF THE SIREN.

He sees a woman, a horrible old hag stuttering, squint-eyed, crooked-legged, sallow-faced, and with both hands frightfully maimed. But something strange suddenly happens.

As Dante keeps staring at her, his very glance performs a miracle. In a matter of seconds the woman, as if obeying Dante's eyes, loses her stammer, straightens herself up, her pallid face acquires the beautiful, rosy color of love, and from her lips begins to flow a music that quickly enchants and enchains

Dante's attention. O happy song!

"I am, I am the Siren sweet,
Who in mid-sea leads mariners astray,
With such delight and bliss am I replete.

I turned Ulysses from his wandering way
With this my song, and he who lives with me—
So much I please him—rarely goes away."

The Siren is still singing when another woman appears—a holy Lady who, wasting no time, bids Virgil expose the filthy temptress. At the Lady's command, Virgil seizes the Siren, rends her clothes, shows her naked belly, and such is the stench that comes out of it that Dante wakes up in horror.

What does this mean?

It means that in Upper Purgatory Dante will meet souls that do penance because of their earthly surrender to the magic of that ancient witch.

But where is the next stairway?

Virgil and Dante see the Holy Mountain adorned with the first shimmer of dawn and begin to walk, their heads still bent beneath the burden of new, mysterious thoughts.

"Come! Here is the stairway."

The ANGEL OF ZEAL, his swanlike wings outspread, brings the two poets to the opening of the solid rock, and then with just a stir of one of his wings erases the fourth P on Dante's brow.

Dante feels relieved, and the ascent is four times easier than it seemed in the beginning, and yet there is sadness in his heart, a strange sadness that has obviously to do with the meaning of his dream.

"What is wrong, that you are still gazing on the ground?" asks Virgil, rebuking him.

"It is the new dream that makes me go on with some suspicion," Dante replies.

"Have you paid attention to the way one has to deal with her? Let that be enough then. And now walk faster— look only to the sky!"

Virgil's words have a magical effect on Dante, who, straightening himself up, climbs the new stairway with reawakened courage.

How beautiful is the new sunrise! But how sad is the sound that comes from the Fifth Cornice!

Who are the new souls lying motionless and outstretched on the ground, so flat on their faces as to seem one with the earth?

CHAPTER NINE
EXCESSIVE LOVE

Bound hands and feet, and prostrate on the pavement of the Fifth Cornice, THE AVARICIOUS and THE PRODIGAL suffer and wail together. On earth they were eager to accumulate or squander wealth, and here in Purgatory they are helplessly fastened to the ground, and therefore compelled to remember what they should have remembered before——that wealth is nothing but dust.

Among these new souls, the first to introduce himself to Dante is POPE ADRIAN V.

Dante was eleven years old when Pope Adrian died only thirty-five days after his election.

"For just a little more than a month," he now tells Dante, "I experienced how heavy the Pope's mantle is on one who wants to keep it unsoiled—so heavy that all other burdens seem feathers.

"My conversion, alas, came late. But as soon as I was made Bishop of Rome, I discovered the falsehood of life. My soul was more than ever unhappy and restless, and as I could soar no higher in my earthly existence, a longing for this true life was therefore kindled in my heart.

"Until then, I had been a wretched soul away from God, and only concerned with material wealth. Now you can see for yourself how I am punished for it.

"But what are you doing? Why did you kneel?"

"Because you were once the Vicar of Christ," replies Dante, full of respect for one whom God had mercifully saved from a long pontificate soiled with avarice and simony. How well he remembers Nicholas III and Boniface VIII!

"Get up! Get up, my brother!" says Adrian in great humility. "There are no Popes here. Like you and like the others, I am a servant of the same Divine Power.

"Go then. I want you to waste no more time, for your tarrying disturbs my weeping."

As Dante leaves Pope Adrian and passes slowly among other weeping souls, he cannot help thinking of the lean and hungry Wolf in the Dark Forest.

"When," he sighs, lifting his glance to the sky, "oh, when will avarice die on man's earth? Oh, when will someone or something come to chase the ravenous Wolf back into Hell?"

Another avaricious soul—HUGH CAPET—tells Dante the story of his life and death, and predicts great misfortunes for his heirs unless they cleanse themselves of the sin of greed.

But, suddenly, the whole Mount of Purgatory shakes. What is happening? So loud is the thunder that the entire Holy Mountain seems for a moment to crumble down from its top.

In terror, Dante turns to Virgil, who promptly reassures him by saying, "Fear not while I am with you."

At this point, singing voices are heard from every side:

"Gloria in excelsis Deo! Glory to God in the highest!"

Standing beside his guide, Dante is in a daze as those shepherds of Bethlehem must have been when they heard the same words sung by the Angels.

But what is it? What is it?

Not even Virgil seems to know.

"God's peace be with you, my brothers."

Quickly, Virgil and Dante turn toward the unexpected voice, and see a soul walking right behind them and not lying down on the floor like all the others in the Fifth Cornice.

"Tell us, if you know," Virgil asks the singular soul, "why the Mountain quaked a while ago, and why all its dwellers seemed to shout in unison."

"The holy regulations of the Mountain," replies the mysterious spirit, "suffer nothing arbitrary or unusual ever to happen...

"The Mountain quakes when, feeling totally cleansed, some soul rises up, eager to fly to Heaven. And at that moment all the others praise God in the highest for that jubilant flight.

"Five hundred years and more have I lain in this torment, but only now have I felt free to long for a better threshold.

"It is for my liberation from this place that you heard the Mountain shake and all the spirits sing."

"Now that I know," says Virgil, "how one suffers and what happens when one is released from this place, will you please tell me who you are and why you had to stay here all these centuries?"

"My name is STATIUS," the happy soul replies, "and I was a famous poet on earth. I wrote the *Thebaid* and the *Achilleid*, though I had no time to complete the latter.

"From that same flame which warmed more than a thousand poets came the spark that lit my own poetic fire—from the *Aeneid*, I mean, which, like a loving mother, nourished my verse. Without the inspiration from that book I would have written nothing at all.

"Oh, to have lived when Virgil was alive, I would gladly postpone by one sun my trip to Heaven!"

At these words, Dante is tempted to reveal to Statius the identity of his beloved guide, but with a stern look Virgil forbids him to do so. "Keep quiet," he seems to say.

Dante remains silent but cannot help smiling.

"Why are you smiling?" Statius asks, baffled.

"Very well, tell him," says Virgil to Dante.

Promptly and proudly, Dante presents to Statius the poet of the *Aeneid*, whereupon the blessed soul, in silent veneration, stoops to embrace Virgil's knees.

"Don't! Don't, my brother!" says Virgil. "A shade you are, and a shade you see."

And so the three poets walk together toward the ascent to the Sixth Cornice. There, on the lowest step of the stairway, the ANGEL OF LIBERALITY strikes the fifth *P* from Dante's brow, thus making him ready to face and bear the next torment up the Mountain.

As he climbs the stairway behind the two Latin poets, he overhears their conversation. Statius tells Virgil that it was prodigality, not avarice, that kept him more than five centuries in the cornice below, and that, had it not been for some prophetic lines in Virgil's works, he would not have become a Christian and would have lost his soul in Hell.

Dante listens to their conversation until his attention is stolen by something quite unexpected—a beautiful tree full of green leaves and sweet, fragrant fruits, and a crystal—clear rivulet flowing down from a rock nearby. From the midst of the green foliage a melodious voice is heard reciting stories that praise the virtue of temperance.

This is the Sixth Cornice, the place where THE GLUTTONS are punished.

They are so thin, so emaciated, that Virgil has the painful impression of looking upon walking skeletons. Their eye-sockets are like rings that have lost their gems, so deeply sunken are their eyes. How can Dante recognize any of them?

But one of them recognizes him, saying, "What grace is this?"

It is FORESE DONATI, an old friend of Dante's.

Poor Forese, so horribly disfigured! He explains to his Florentine friend that in this cornice all the new souls sanctify themselves by suffering hunger and thirst. The sweet scent that comes from the tree makes them hungry, and the sound of the flowing water makes them thirsty. And so around that tree and around that spring they go and go, every time hungrier and thirstier, but unable and unwilling to relieve their torment.

But Dante is hardly listening. He is remembering a very dark and wicked period in his life. Almost five years have elapsed since the day of Forese's death, but he cannot forget how unjust he once was to him. They had vehemently quarreled and, worse, even insulted each other in the most vulgar fashion. But he, Dante, had doubtless been the more cruel of the two when, to make his insult more stinging and venomous, he had dragged an innocent person into their fight — Forese's charming, pious young wife, Nella.

"Tell me, Forese," asks Dante, "how did you get up here so soon? Should you not be below, outside the Gate, having turned to God at the last moment of your life?'

Forese's reply is as quick as it is gentle:

"It was my Nella who helped me with her incessant tears. Because of her saintly prayers I was allowed to climb to my cornice long before my time.

"The more lonely she is in good deeds, the dearer to God is my darling little widow I loved so well. . . . Ah, today those shameless, brazen-faced women of Florence go around exhibiting their breasts."

The mention of Nella's name causes Dante to say, not without a tinge of embarrassment:

"If you recall how we behaved toward each other, the present memory will still be painful. But from that kind of life I have been saved by the one who walks before me. He led me, soul and body, through the Deep Night in order to save me from those who are truly dead. . . . He will stay with me until I come to the place where I shall meet Beatrice...

"He is Virgil. The other is the one for whose discharge the whole Mountain quaked a while ago — Statius, I mean, who, perhaps to keep Virgil company, is delaying the beginning of his eternal happiness."

Not yet realizing that he is being stared at by the souls who have overheard his words "soul and body," Dante asks about Forese's sister, Piccarda.

"My good and lovely sister is already in Heaven," answers Forese.

"And who are these, who keep staring at me?"

"That one over there is Bonagiunta.

BONAGIUNTA ORBICCIANI, a poet from Lucca, addresses Dante with great respect and, to please him more, even quotes the first line of one of his poems.

Dante is still listening to Bonagiunta when he sees all the souls leap toward a tree, another tree in full bloom at the other end of the cornice. Only Forese remains behind to ask something else of Dante.

"When shall I see you again?"

"I don't know how much longer I am expected to live," Dante replies, "but one thing is sure: my desire will come back here long before my spirit does, for the place where I live becomes day by day more wicked, and seems doomed to fatal ruin."

Finally, Forese joins his fellow sufferers, and Dante now can see them all beneath the new tree, lifting up their arms toward its fruit-laden branches like little greedy children who beg and beg in vain.

That is a shoot from the ancient tree from which Eve picked the fruit of all evil.

Virgil, Dante, and Statius are walking slowly, listening to the singing voices coming out of the green leaves, when someone says to them "What are you three thinking about?"

Dante looks up and sees the ANGEL OF TEMPERANCE in the fullness of his red-glowing glory.

"If you want to climb farther, here is where you must turn," he tells the three pilgrims. Then, he erases the sixth *P* on Dante's brow with a touch of his wing, which wafts, as it moves, such a fragrance as to make Dante think of the sweet breeze on a May morning.

And now it is time to climb to the last cornice.

In the Seventh Cornice THE LUSTFUL cleanse themselves in fire. The place is all one smoky conflagration, except for a narrow ledge on which the poets must carefully walk in single file.

The difference between the torments of Hell and those of Purgatory is that in Hell the souls ask in vain for some respite, whereas in Purgatory they are happy to suffer, and therefore are careful not to lose one instant of their precious suffering.

That is why, though gathering in amazement in front of Dante whose shadow makes the flames look redder, the Lustful are eager not to leave, even for one second, the fire that burns them.

One of them—GUIDO GUINIZELLI—introduces himself to Dante, who upon hearing the name of his favorite Tuscan poet, feels like leaping into the flames to embrace him.

It is he who explains the identity of the second group of souls he has just seen

The lustful.

96

coming from the other side of the cornice and kissing one another in the midst of the flames. "We are," he says, "those who sinned against nature, whereas the others have only sinned against man's social institutions."

Dante tells Guinizelli how much he admires his poetry.

"Brother," answers Guinizelli, "that man over there was a much better craftsman in his mother tongue than I in mine."

After these words, the poet from Bologna disappears into the thick of the flames, like a fish going downward to the bottom of the sea.

The "better craftsman" introduces himself as ARNAUT DANIEL, a great Provençal poet who died sixty-five years before Dante was born. Speaking the Provençal tongue, he asks Dante to pray for him.

The ANGEL OF CHASTITY removes the seventh and last P from Dante's brow, and tells the three poets to go through the flames and climb the final steps of the Mountain.

Thus comes to an end the third day in Purgatory—a day spent among souls guilty of excessive love for things that should have been secondary in their earthly existence— pursuit of wealth, pleasures of the table, and carnal appetite.

"All right, my son," says Virgil, "let us go through these flames, as the Angel commands."

Go through the flames and become a heap of ashes? Dante hesitates.

"Don't you trust me?" Virgil insists. "If I guided you safely on the back of Geryon, what shall I do now that you are nearer to God?"

But Dante is still stubborn and silent.

"My son," says Virgil, "between you and Beatrice there is but this wall. So, do you still wish to stay here?"

At the name of Beatrice, Dante feels suddenly ready to brave a thousand flames, and Virgil smiles as one does at a child who has finally been conquered by an apple.

Through the last purifying flames the three poets go toward the stairway leading to the Garden of Eden on top of the Mountain.

They climb several steps until the darkness of the new night comes and they must interrupt their ascent and wait for the sun.

Resting his head on one of the steps, Dante falls into a slumber filled with thoughts of Beatrice, so near at last.

At daybreak, he has a dream—THE DREAM OF LEAH. He sees in his dream a Lady, young and fair, gathering flowers along a lovely meadow. "I am Leah," she says, "and with these hands I am weaving myself a garland. Here I am making myself beautiful so that I may look at myself with joy in the mirror. But my sister Rachel looks at herself in the mirror all day, as delighted in gazing at her own fair eyes as I am in adorning myself with blossoms. She finds her happiness in contemplation, I find mine in action."

What a beautiful dream, but what does it mean? When Dante wakes up, he sees the new light all about him, and the two masters ready to climb the remaining steps.

"My son," says Virgil, "I have brought you here with wisdom and art. Now let your own happiness be your guide, for you are out of the steep and narrow paths. Look at the sun shining ahead! Look at the tender grass, and at the flowers and shrubs which this ground brings forth of itself!

"Until she comes, whose tearful eyes made me speed to your rescue, you can sit here or go there into all that beauty.

"Do not expect my word or my signal any longer. Your will is free, upright, and self-sufficient: now it would be your fault alone not to act according to its counseling.

"I crown and miter you master of yourself."

If Dante only knew that by telling him that from now on he is completely on his own, Virgil has just bidden him goodbye!

It is Wednesday morning after Easter.

CHAPTER TEN
THE EARTHLY PARADISE

Such is the entrancing beauty of this new place that without even saying a word of thanks to Virgil, Dante starts walking into it.

This is THE DIVINE FOREST, the forest, that is, which God himself had planted for the first man. In the lovely greenness of these trees Adam had once been innocent and happy.

How beautiful is every corner of it, and how sweet the air one breathes! A soft breeze, indicative of an eternal morning, comes to caress Dante's forehead and makes every leaf gently bend toward that side of the Mountain on which the first shadow is already resting.

And what songs, what carefree music in the air! Unafraid of storm and winter, birds keep singing on every branch, on every tree, and with lower, mellower notes the morning air itself re-echoes all their melodies.

Oh, rapture of sound and color! As if all this were not enough, a tremulous rivulet flows, bending the ever—young, ever—green grasses along its banks. The clearest stream on earth is muddy in comparison. Yet, forever flowing under the forever shading foliage of the Forest, this rivulet seems to be dark, quite dark.

Utterly entranced, Dante feels like crossing the lovely current at once, but he checks his burning desire. On its opposite bank he sees, suddenly, so many flowers that he thinks of past, present, and future Mays blossoming all at once in that one spot of the world. And there, too, on the same bank, amid all those flowers, he sees MATILDA, a beautiful lady whose charm and gracefulness vanquish all other wonders as she moves gathering bud after bud and sweetly singing.

"O beautiful lady," Dante cries out, "oh, please, come closer so that I may hear the song you are singing."

Like a dancing figure coming nimbly on tiptoe to the foreground of a stage, the luminous lady comes toward Dante, who finally is able to understand the words of her song.

She stops three paces across from him on the right bank of the stream, still gathering flower after flower. Her eyes are so lovely and bright they defy a poet's description.

"You are newcomers here," she says, turning to Virgil, Statius, and Dante, "and so perhaps you're wondering why I am smiling in this place where mankind was destined to live.

"But you," she says to Dante alone, "you who begged me to come, and are now standing in front of me, if you have questions to ask, this is the time, for I am ready to please you."

Dante is baffled by the nature of the breeze and the stream in this Divine Forest.

Matilda tells him that the breeze in the Garden of Eden is not caused, as in the lower part of the atmosphere, by the vapors of the earth, but is, instead, one with the circular motion of the air that strikes the top of the Mountain.

The stream, Matilda also explains, does not come from any source fed by mist or rain as is the case with all rivers and rivulets on earth. It flows from a steady, smooth, eternal Spring which, in turn, takes its supplies from God's will itself.

"The ancient poets," Matilda concludes, "who wrote about the Golden Age and its happy state, dreamed perhaps of this place when they mentioned Mount Parnassus."

"Here the root of man's race was innocent. Here is spring everlasting, and every kind of fruit. Here is the nectar everyone talks about."

At these words, Virgil and Statius, two of those "ancient poets," smile.

Though enraptured in Matilda's world, Dante notices that Virgil, his beloved guide, is still there with him. But does he know that he will soon lose him forever?

Soaring from rapture to higher rapture, Dante begins to follow the beautiful lady, keeping pace with her on the left bank of the stream. The new song Matilda sings makes him fully aware of the meaning of the Earthly Paradise. Oh, why, why was Eve so bold as to disobey God's word? If she had not sinned, this would be man's home forever.

A tiny stream separates Matilda from Dante, but the same ecstasy unites them: one, so to speak, is the music, and the other its echo.

How long has Dante been following Matilda into the peaceful Forest? He himself cannot tell. He only knows that something else is happening, something wonderful and mysterious.

"Brother, look! Listen!" Matilda says suddenly, turning to Dante.

An unexpected brightness seems at this moment to run through the Forest. "What can this be?" thinks Dante, astonished. It cannot be a flash of lightning, for, instead of abating and disappearing, the unusual splendor grows by the minute larger and deeper —a flood of whiteness vanquishing all other colors about.

And a sweet melody runs through the luminous air, outsinging birds and breeze. What can this be? thinks Dante, astounded.

And his amazement grows when he sees, a little farther on, seven trees of gold walking toward him from the other side of the Forest. As they come nearer, he realizes that they are not walking trees but SEVEN FLAMING CANDELABRA held aloft by nearly invisible figures singing "Hosanna."

Dante turns to his dear Virgil for some explanation but Virgil replies with a baffled glance that seems to say, "All this is beyond my understanding. Didn't I tell you that you must now rely on yourself?"

Virgil is still there, but as far as his counseling is concerned, it is as though he were not there with him at all. His mission is over—it had come to an end on the Seventh Cornice.

"Why are you so taken by the vision of these seven flaming lights, and do not look at what is coming behind them?"

Gently rebuked by Matilda, Dante looks behind the Seven Candelabra, following the seven trails of light that look like seven colorful rainbows.

This is only the beginning of the mysterious parade.

TWENTY-FOUR ELDERS advance in majestic solemnity, two by two, and all clad in white. They seem to be singing.

As they come a little closer, Dante can hear distinctly the words of the hymn they are singing: "Blessèd art thou amongst women."

Dante looks at them with keen attention, trying to understand the meaning of their number. He knows that Virgil cannot help him any longer, and it is now his own responsibility to see how and why all these wonders are happening around him. Could it be that Beatrice is soon to appear? Who sent Matilda to him, and what is the meaning of her presence in the Earthly Paradise? Why seven candelabra? Why twenty-four elders? Why white, and not brown or gray? And why that particular hymn and not another?

Later — the answers will come later. The Mystical Procession continues, and there is no time to lose.

After the Twenty-four Elders, Dante sees FOUR BEASTS, each crowned with green leaves and plumed with six wings full of eyes. The air is calm and bright, and yet it seems that each of these four mysterious animals carries wind and mist and fire along.

In the midst of them a TRIUMPHAL CHARIOT advances on two wheels, drawn by a GRIFFON, an animal half lion and half eagle with limbs half of gold and half of white mingled with vermilion.

So beautiful is this Chariot that that of the Sun or of the greatest Roman emperor is in comparison a very common cart indeed.

By its right wheel, THREE LADIES come dancing: one dressed in red, another in green, and the last in snowy white.

By the Chariot's left wheel, not three but FOUR LADIES are seen in a festive mood, all clad in purple with one of them flashing not two but three bright eyes.

Not far behind the Chariot, TWO MORE ELDERS advance, unlike in their attire, but alike in their bearing, and both dignified and venerable. One looks like a physician; the other, with a sharp and glittering sword in hand, gives Dante a sudden sense of fear.

At the end of the Procession, FIVE MORE ELDERS walk slowly and humbly, all dressed in white like the first twenty-four, but, unlike them, wearing around their brows wreaths of red flowers instead of white. The last of them, coming somewhat behind the others, has the face of a man utterly lost in a dream.

What can all these figures mean? Surely they must mean something or God's grace would not display them to Dante's eyes.

The Seven Candelabra signify the Seven Moral Virtues one achieves as one is cleansed of the Seven Capital Sins.

The Seven Rainbows signify the Seven Sacraments.

The first Twenty-four Elders represent the twenty-four books of the Old Testament.

The Four Beasts represent the Four Gospels.

The Triumphal Chariot represents the Church in her victorious journey, and the Griffon with its double nature of lion and eagle symbolizes Christ in His human and divine nature.

The Three Ladies by the right wheel of the Chariot are the Three Theological Virtues — Charity, Hope, and Faith.

The Four Ladies by the left wheel of the Chariot are the Four Cardinal Virtues — Prudence, Justice, Temperance, and Fortitude.

The Seven Elders are, respectively, the Apostles Luke, Paul, James, Peter, Jude, John, and, finally, Saint Bernard if not Moses himself or even the very symbol of the Apocalypse.

Dante is still trying hard not to miss the least detail of the wondrous Pageant when a sudden thunderclap makes the entire Procession stop.

Elders and Ladies turn to face the Chariot. Is Beatrice coming?

CHAPTER ELEVEN

HUMILIATION, TEARS, AND HAPPINESS

"Come, O Bride, from Lebanon!"

At these mysterious words, uttered by one of the Elders, a hundred Angels appear around the Triumphal Chariot, casting lilies above and about it.

Finally, a Lady is seen standing on the left side of the Chariot. Her dress is the color of a living flame, her mantle is green, and she wears an olive wreath over her white veil.

There can be no doubt who she is.

It is not possible to gaze on the face of the sun unless it rises somewhat shadowed by the presence of the morning mists.

Because of the ample shower of petals falling from the angelic hands, Dante is able to gaze, without being completely dazzled, on the face of the beautiful, mysterious woman. Suddenly, his heart beats faster, and he grows afraid. After twenty-five years he feels as he felt when at the age of only nine he met a girl called Beatrice. He re-experiences in his heart and mind the wonder and fear of that first moment of love.

Like a little child running to his mother for help, he turns to Virgil, saying, "I recognize the traces of the ancient flame." But Virgil— oh, where is he?

Virgil is gone, Virgil his sweet father, Virgil his trusted savior.

There are tears in Dante's eyes now that he sees himself abandoned by his beloved Master. In a flash he recalls how many times his kind, affectionate Teacher had saved him from danger through the dark City of the Dead. Where would he be without Virgil? He would have died in the Dark Forest. And what would he have done at the Gate of the City of Dis if Virgil had not told him of the coming of a Messenger from Heaven? Who would have carried him up the most dangerous slopes in the Circles of Hell? And even now, in Purgatory, what would he have replied to Cato and the Angel of the Church if Virgil had not answered for him? 0 Virgil, dear Virgil!

Dante is crying, and there is a mixture of sorrow, gratitude, and anxiety in the bitterness of his tears. Suddenly too sad, not only does he remember Virgil's last words but he also realizes that there cannot be any room for a pagan in this realm of Christian faith and belief. Human reason cannot understand the mysteries of Revelation; it can only lead through an objective analysis of sin and sinner to the threshold of beatitude, but not beyond.

"Dante," a voice is heard at this point, "don't cry for your loss of Virgil. Oh, don't cry, don't cry yet. It is for something worse that you must cry."

Dante recognizes the voice.

"Yes, look at me well. I am, I am Beatrice. So, you have climbed the Mountain at last! Did you not know that only here can one be happy?"

Dante drops his eyes, heavy with shame, to the limpid stream.

Why is Beatrice so stern, so harsh, so cruel to the one she loves? Or does she not love him any more? Oh, she loves him still. She loves him more than ever now that he is cleansed of all his sins. Does a mother love her child less when she scolds him for something that he should not have done?

The hundred Angels between Dante and Beatrice try to plead for him whose glance is still bent by the remembrance of his wicked past, but Beatrice is none the less determined to teach Dante the most painful lesson of his life.

"Your eyes are bright with the Eternal Day," she replies to them, "and you are not affected by the evil ways of the world below. That is why I must speak to that man weeping beyond the stream. I want his sorrow to be as great as his sin.

Beatrice.

"He had, in his prime, such potential greatness in him that all his good talents would surely have reached magnificent heights. But the better and more vigorous the soil, the worse and more wild it grows if sown with evil seed and left untilled.

"For some time I encouraged him with my presence: showing my youthful eyes to him, I led him toward his noble goal.

"But as soon as I was on the threshold of my second age, and started my new life, he forgot all about me and turned elsewhere.

"When I arose from flesh to spirit, and beauty and virtue grew within me, he found me less attractive and dear, and started to walk on the wrong path, pursuing false visions of good.

"It was no use obtaining inspiration for him, with which in dream and otherwise I called and called him back: so little did he care about it.

"So low he sank that all means for his salvation had already proved useless, save showing him the people lost in Hell.

"For this I visited the Gate of Death, and offered my tears and prayers to the one who guided him up here.

"God's high command would be broken if one were to cross the River Lethe and taste of our bliss without any shedding of tears of penance."

Turning to Dante, blushing and weeping on the other bank of the stream, Beatrice says, her voice a piercing needle:

"Speak up, speak up: is this true? Let your own confession answer such charges against you.

"What now? Answer me, for the sad memories of your past have not yet been erased by the water."

Confusion and fear, together mingled, cause Dante to plead guilty in the presence of the woman who can read all his thoughts.

"Yes," he replies in a whisper.

"At the time you used to long for me," Beatrice retorts, "you were spurred by your desire to love only that Good beyond which there is nothing else to crave. But then , what pitfalls or what chains did you find along your path that made you stop in terror? And what allurements, what advantages did you see on other women's faces to wander, enchanted, around them?"

Heaving a bitter sigh, and groping for words, Dante answers:

"Things of the world with their false pleasure turned my steps away as soon as your face was concealed from my eyes."

"If you were silent," Beatrice continues, "or if you had denied what you have just confessed, do you think you would hide your guilt from us? You cannot cheat God's Judgment.

"But in our Court self-accusation is most meritorious. However, so that you may now feel ashamed of your mistake, and be stronger, when you hear the Sirens again, stop crying, and listen. I will tell you how my death should have led you to a different goal.

"Never did nature and art present to you so great a bliss as the fair body which was my home for awhile, and now is only dust. And if my death made you lose sight of the highest happiness, what mortal thing could have prompted you to yearn for it?

105

"At that first proof of the deception of all earthly things you should have risen, instead, after me, who was no longer one of them. But you allowed such a thing as a pretty young face to weigh your wings down with the brief pleasure it gave you....

"Now lift up your chin, and look at me."

So complete is Dante's humiliation that he is afraid of gazing on Beatrice. Oh, how he wishes he had never looked on the unworthy things of the world!

"Look at me! Look at me!"

It is much easier to uproot an oak from its rocky ground than to convince Dante to raise his eyes from the limpid stream.

Finally, he looks up, and sees Beatrice facing Christ, symbolized by the Griffon.

How beautiful she is! How much more beautiful than she ever was in her mortal day!

How long can Dante bear the beauty of those eyes? Love and remorse are so strong in his heart that he falls to the ground like a lifeless weight. When he comes to, Beatrice is no longer in front of him. But what is happening?

Dante finds himself in the RIVER LETHE with its waves up to his neck. Is he drowning?

Matilda, the beautiful lady who a while ago was gathering flowers along the bank of the stream, is over him, saying, "Hold on to me! Hold on to me!"

Finally, opening her arms, she seizes him by the head and dips him into the stream, thus forcing him to swallow some of the water.

Moments later, Dante finds himself on the bank, surrounded by four lovely nymphs and caught up in their graceful dance.

Who are they? Where did they come from? What are they singing?

Here only nymphs, we are bright stars in heaven;
Long before Beatrice on earth descended
We were to her as humble handmaids given.

We to her eyes will lead you; but those three
Who on the other side are closer to her
Will make you her deep light more deeply see.

Dante is beginning to understand. He is being brought before Beatrice by the Four Cardinal Virtues, who, in turn, beg the Three Theological Virtues to ask their gentle mistress to unveil her eyes to him.

Turn, Beatrice, oh, turn your holy gaze

To your beloved faithful man who came,
To see you, through so many thorny ways.

To make us happy, oh, to him reveal
The sweetness of your mouth, that he may see
The second beauty that you still conceal.

Beatrice unveils her face, and smiles. Who can describe this moment of happiness?

Happy and filled with wonderment, Dante's soul seems to taste of some supernatural food that at the same time both satisfies and whets its hunger.

Ten years, ten long years have elapsed since the day of Beatrice's death, and now here she is at last, more beautiful than ever, more merciful than ever, and forever part of his life, forever his entire life.

The water of the River Lethe has made him forget all his past, has washed away every sad memory of sin.

Now all is new, all is pure, all is bright. It is as if Adam had never sinned and therefore never left this place of splendor.

If this is only paradise on earth, what will God's Paradise be like?

CHAPTER TWELVE
THE HORRIBLE VISION

When Dante removes his eyes from the splendor of Beatrice's holy smile, he sees the Mystical Procession move slowly eastward.

Dante and Statius (oh, where is Virgil?) follow Matilda behind the Triumphal Chariot, drawn once again by the double-natured Griffon.

Where is the Divine Pageant going? Through the lofty Forest, so empty on account of Eve's surrender to the Serpent, now moves the Holy Parade.

Where is everyone going? After a while, everyone stops in front of THE MYSTICAL TREE—the tall tree of the Knowledge of Good and Evil, now utterly devoid of flowers and the different-colored foliage which once adorned its boughs.

The Griffon does not break the tree, whereupon a universal song of praise is heard:

"O blessed Griffon, who with your beak do not rend this tree whose fruit is so sweet to taste!"

To Dante's amazement, the Griffon replies:

"Thus is preserved the seed of justice." Dante understands at once that the Mystical Tree symbolizes God's Justice, which no one must approach with disrespect. What he fails to understand is the Griffon's next movement.

The Holy Beast, fully aware of its mission, turns toward the Tree, draws the Chariot under it, and binds it to its trunk.

Wonder of wonders! As soon as the Chariot touches the barren trunk, the Tree revives, and its sudden life makes every branch grow green and beautiful again.

A new song of praise is sung by all the blessed souls, but Dante, too deeply dazed by the new light coming out of the Tree, falls into a slumber and dreams of Christ's Blood giving new life and beauty to every barren tree.

When he awakens, he feels like Peter, James, and John after the Transfiguration of Jesus on Mount Tabor.

What has happened during his brief slumber?

Where are all the blessed souls?

"Where is Beatrice?" Dante asks with a painful sensation of solitude and abandonment.

"There she is, sitting upon the roots of the newly adorned Tree," answers Matilda.

Dante raises his eyes, and sees his beloved Beatrice at the foot of the Tree, surrounded by the Seven Virtues. All the other blessed souls, including the Holy

Griffon, have soared to Heaven, singing a song of sweet and deep enchantment.

Why is Beatrice so lonely at the foot of the Tree? Is she the only guardian of the abandoned Chariot?

The Seven Ladies are around her, each holding a lighted taper to shed light upon the Forest. But why is Beatrice so lonely at the foot of the Mystical Tree? And why is she guarding it as if some danger were imminent?

Turning to Dante, "Here in this Forest," she says, "you will stay a little longer, and then you will forever be a citizen, like me, of that Rome in which Christ, too, is a Roman."

A little longer, and Dante will be with Beatrice in Heaven.

"But," Beatrice continues, "for the benefit of the world that lives in sin, keep your eyes fixed on the Chariot, and when you go back on earth, see that you write what you are about to witness."

What will happen?

Dante would surely be afraid of his task were it not for Beatrice's assuring words, "you will forever be a citizen, like me, of that Rome in which Christ, too, is a Roman."

Keeping his eyes fixed on the Chariot bound to the Tree, Dante is ready for the new mysterious happenings.

Like fire breaking out of a thick cloud, the EAGLE OF PERSECUTION swoops suddenly down upon the Tree, rends its bark, ruins its flowers and its new leaves, and smites the Chariot with such fury that, like a vessel beaten by the waves of a stormy sea, it crumbles on its two wheels.

Dante gasps, utterly powerless in the contemplation of the Church being persecuted by the Empire, and of the Tree of God's Justice being so gravely offended.

Before he can look at Beatrice for some explanation, the FOX OF HERESY leaps into the body of the Triumphal Chariot, eager to sate her hunger. But Beatrice, indignant at the new profanation suffered by Holy Mother Church, chases the famished animal away with the power of her mystical presence.

The same Eagle comes down again, and this time it leaves some of its feathers strewn over the Chariot. At once, Dante thinks of Constantine, the Roman Emperor who on becoming a Christian gave the Pope a bit of land as a token of his gratitude—a gift that was to bring more harm than good to the Church. That is why Dante now hears a mysterious lamenting voice saying, "O my little ship, what dangerous merchandise you are carrying!"

And now—look!—the earth opens between the two wheels of the Chariot, and a DRAGON, Satan himself, comes out of the gaping hole and flings his tail over the Chariot.

What is the meaning of this sudden horrible abyss between the two wheels of the Chariot? It means that the unity of the Church will soon be broken by several schisms such as the one wrought by Mohammed, and that the Devil will seem to triumph over the ruins of the Christian world.

Dante looks, terrified, at the devastation of the Church, but the horrid vision is not yet over.

In less time than it takes a man to say "oh," the few feathers left by the Imperial Eagle in its second flight begin to multiply until they cover the still visible parts of the Chariot. In other words, that bit of land which the Pope accepted from Constantine grows and grows into a vast wealth, which fully covers and hides the real meaning and mission of the Church. No one can recognize Christ any more beneath the treacherous adornments of His Church.

The Chariot has become a monstrous building all entangled with luscious, poisonous leaves, and seven horrible heads appear on top of it—three on what was the pole of the Chariot, and one at each corner. They are the Seven Capital Sins—the only things left for the Church to show mankind.

Sprawled on the roof of this monstrous architecture, a HARLOT and a GIANT embrace each other shamelessly under the eyes of the whole world.

Who are they? Is the Harlot the Roman Curia, and the Giant the King of France? Whoever they are, is this the kind of thing a Christian has to expect from the Church of Rome? Has the Mystical Body of Christ become, then, a filthy object of prostitution?

Dante feels like burying his face in his hands so as to spare himself the horror of the unspeakable sacrilege, but he remembers Beatrice's warning, "When you go back on earth, see that you write what you are about to witness."

Oh, why doesn't Beatrice do something to stop this atrocious act of profanation and save the Church for the future of mankind? And why does God in Heaven allow all this evil to triumph on man's earth?

Each moment seems an eternity.

Speechless and powerless, Beatrice can only look at what has become of Rome and the Roman Church. But there is the same bright light in her eyes, which is like the sun that strikes on the mud of the earth and remains unsoiled and pure. Is it hope? Is it certainty of future victories?

Suddenly, the Giant rises to his feet, and to punish the Harlot for turning toward Dante, begins to scourge her mercilessly from head to toe.

Then the Giant jumps down from the top of the horrible building and does something to it, whereupon the seven heads are seen to move, and the entire structure becomes the back of a huge beast.

This monster is now being dragged by the Giant through the deserted Forest.

It seems that the power of Hell has prevailed at last. The Seven Virtues are in tears.

Beatrice is desolate and pale: she looks like Mary at the foot of the Cross.

It is the black hour of Christ's Crucifixion. When will the glorious morning of His Resurrection shine on the world?

Soon, very soon.

The Giant and the Harlot.

CHAPTER THIRTEEN
THE LAST MOMENTS ON THE EARTH

"A little while, and ye shall not see me: and again, a little while, and ye shall see me, because I go to the Father."

With the very words with which Christ comforted his disciples before his ascension to Heaven, Beatrice comforts the Seven Virtues, her sweet handmaids, in tears.

It means that she, too, is soon to return to the Father. Will she take Dante along and show him God's Paradise at last, after so much anguish, so much fright?

Preceded by the Seven Virtues and followed by Matilda, Dante, and Statius, Beatrice starts walking toward the other end of the Earthly Paradise, a brighter light of hope and victory in her holy eyes.

After less than ten steps, she turns to Dante, saying:

"Come closer, so that if I talk to you, you may listen to me better."

Dante moves forward and walks right beside her. "Now that you are with me," she says with a tender, tranquil smile, "why don't you ask me all the questions you wanted to ask before?"

Love and reverence make Dante grope for words.

"My Lady," he answers, "you know all my needs, and what can satisfy them."

"Very well," Beatrice continues. "I want you to disentangle yourself from your last fear and shame. Only then will you be able to speak like a man no longer dreaming.

"Remember my words: the Chariot broken by the Dragon was, and is not. Corrupt as she is now, the Church of Christ is as though she were no more. But tell those who are responsible for all this harm that God's vengeance fears no one.

"Yet not forever will the Imperial Eagle be absent. I can already see, close to their birth, new stars free from every obstacle or impediment.

"A Messenger of God will be sent to kill the Giant now misbehaving with the Church.

"Though what I am telling you may now sound obscure, pay attention, and just as I convey them to you, convey my words among those who live and die on earth.

"And do not forget to tell them how you saw the Tree of the Knowledge of Good and Evil, devastated first by the Eagle of Persecution and now by the Giant that is dragging it, along with the remnants of the Chariot, through the empty Forest.

"He who robs or rends that Tree, with his blasphemous act offends God, who created it holy and only for His service.

"But because I see your intellect turned to stone by futile thoughts, and even stained by the pleasure they used to give you, I want my words to remain, if not carved in you, at least as a painted remembrance of your journey."

The more Dante tries to understand the meaning of Beatrice's beloved words, the more obscure he finds them. But his mind, he feels, is like wax on which things are being stamped which he will understand and look at later.

"A painted remembrance of your journey." Does this mean that his journey is over? Will Beatrice return to God without him? Will he not see, then, as Virgil promised in the Dark Forest a long, long time ago, "the Blessed Souls in Heaven"?

The decision rests with Beatrice, the "worthier soul," as Virgil called her then.

But is he worthy of climbing to the Stars with her? "I don't recall," he says to her, "ever straying away from you, nor is there any memory in me that bothers my conscience."

"Of course," Beatrice replies, with a smile, "you have just drunk of Lethe—the water that washes away all evil remembrances. Yet, just as smoke is indicative of fire, the very fact that you do not remember clearly proves that something has been forgotten. But from now on my words will be simple and therefore easy for your mind to grasp."

The small group has meanwhile come to the end of the Earthly Paradise, all flooded with the light of the noonday sun.

Everything grows brighter except a tiny part of the ground that looks like a shadow—it is the place where two rivulets are born—LETHE and EUNÔE.

Why do the Seven Ladies stop right there, near the limpid water?

"O light, O glory of all mankind," Dante asks Beatrice, "what water is this that here pours forth from one source, and then flows in two different directions?"

"Ask Matilda about it," replies Beatrice.

"I have already told him about the nature of the streams of this Forest," Matilda explains, "and I hope that Lethe's water has not canceled his memory of it."

"Perhaps because of the many incredible things he has seen he has forgotten all about it," Beatrice says in his favor. "But look, there is Eunöe sweetly flowing. Take him there, and as you are accustomed to do, revive his fainting virtue."

Making Beatrice's wish her own, Matilda takes Dante by the hand, and most affably says to Statius, "You come too."

How can one describe the sweet taste of the water of Eunöe?

He who drinks of it suddenly remembers the good of all his actions. That is why, tasting of the sacred waves, Dante at this moment recalls only the good of his past deeds and of his journey so far.

113

He recalls his own praise of Beatrice when, in the Dark Forest, Virgil had told him of her coming down to Limbo for his sake. He recalls how, to save himself from death, he trusted Virgil with all his heart. He remembers the moment when an Angel came down from Heaven to open the Gate of the City of Dis. He remembers the wonderful kindness of a soul called Pia de' Tolomei, the warmth of Sordello, the beauty and gentleness of Matilda, and most of all, the words of his dear, dear Beatrice.

He remembers all the good things Heaven wants him to remember for the salvation of his soul, just as he has forgotten—thanks to the water of Lethe—all the unpleasantness and ugliness of sin.

His mind is free of all memories of guilt while his heart is full of remembrances of love and beauty. As he drinks avidly of Eunõe at Matilda's invitation, he feels like a long-dead tree suddenly reblooming.

Oh, now he knows that his journey is not over. Beatrice will take him along from heaven to heaven until he sees and feels what no other living man has ever seen and felt before—God's infinite light and love.

When will the happy flight begin?
Is Beatrice nodding?
One thing is sure: he feels cleansed and ready, at last, to climb to the Stars.

The River Eunõe.

Paradise

CHAPTER ONE
HEAVEN OF THE MOON: THE LOGIC OF WEIGHTLESSNESS

The glory of the One Who moves all things
cleaves through the universe and everywhere
in different degrees its splendor brings.

There in that heaven where his light is brightest,
was I, and saw what no one ever could,
or would know how to render manifest,

for, coming closer to its longed-for good,
founders our intellect in such a measure
that memory fails to follow as it would.

And yet the faintest glimmer I could treasure
of all that Blissful Kingdom in my mind
will now inspire my singing with its pleasure.

Beatrice raises her gaze to the light above, and so does Dante. He notices that her glance, instead of being dazzled by the flaming radiance of the sun, can almost subdue it. The earth, the frightful earth of his past, looks so distant, so small that it causes him to wonder how he has climbed so high in less than an instant. Beatrice is there with him, aware of his apprehension, and smiling at his wonderment. But where are they now?

They are in the Sphere of Fire, on their way to the Heaven of the Moon.

Dante feels like a new person. His human nature, while still retaining all the characteristics of its mortality, experiences such a joyful sensation of weightlessness that he can only compare himself to Glaucus. Glaucus, one day, having tasted some herb on the shore, fell so deeply in love with the sea that, spurred by an inexplicable impulse, he jumped into the waves and became part of it forever.

But how can one explain one's sudden transhumanation? From this moment hence, Dante must try to remember that he will soar from heaven to heaven with the same natural ease with which a river flows down to the sea. His motion, from now on, will no longer remind him of things that speed toward death but of spheres that revolve around God's endless life. But how can he think in divine terms if he is a merely mortal man capable only of believing the things he comprehends? Or is this new sensation nothing but deception? Is he in heaven, soul and body, or with his soul alone?

Beatrice, who can read Dante's thoughts, explains to him: "It is your old habits of thinking that make it hard for you to believe what you see. You are no longer on earth."

"But how can I," Dante asks, baffled, "transcend all the light bodies circling around me?"

Heaving a patient, affectionate sigh, Beatrice answers: "Order keeps all things together, and that is why the universe is made in the image of God... Order attracts all things, each in its own instinctive way... Unfortunately, however, there are men who willingly detach themselves from it... Do not marvel, then, at your climbing, which is as natural as the downward course of a river. Do you expect a lively flame to stay idle on the ground? Then why do you, who now are cleansed and free, wish to remain inactive on the earth?"

The noonday sun is now so bright that a second daylight seems to be added to the first. The Creator of the world, it seems, has suddenly adorned the firmament with a second, more dazzling sun. If this is only an imperfect glimpse of God's immortal splendor, what will His face be like, nine heavens away?

> You that in a small vessel follow me,
> borne by desire to listen to my song
> as my ship onward furrows the deep sea,
>
> return to the safe shore where you belong;
> forget the perilous ocean, for if me
> you lose, you'll be lost also before long.

The reader has been warned: if he is afraid to follow, let him row back to the shore. But how can one who has seen such luminous day above the day return to the darkness below?

Dante follows Beatrice's example. He, too, gazes heavenward until they are both in the HEAVEN OF THE MOON. Here a bright, thick cloud, like a diamond pierced by the sun, envelops Beatrice and Dante, who once more begins to wonder what is happening around him. He is grateful to God, Whose power has lifted him from the mortal world; but, now that he is on the Moon, he is still far from comprehending the lunar marks that men on earth believe to be the sinister shadow of Cain, the first murderer.

Beatrice smiles, and tells him that, contrary to what man's reason believes, the lunar stains are caused by the fact that the power of God reveals itself in various degrees throughout His universe. He is made to understand the very

117

secret of the bliss of the heavenly spirits. They are with God forever, but from now on they will appear to Dante in seven different planets whose different velocity bespeaks the degree of their eternal peace. It is as though a happy monarch, seated on an invisible throne thousands of miles away, projected his image through a mirror placed at the end of a measureless corridor.

As in more mirrors of transparent hue,
or deep in waters, undisturbed and clear,
of which our gaze the bottom still can view,

we see our very features as a mere
perlaceous color on a pallid brow—
a faint and formless sight we almost fear—

so many a face eager to talk I saw.

In the diaphanous mist of the Moon several souls are seen. They are the INCONSTANT SPIRITS, those who were not steadfast in their religious life on earth. They all seem eager to speak to Dante, who, finally, says to one of them: "O soul created for unending bliss, which only those can fathom who dwell in it, oh, tell me who you are and how you live here in Heaven."

PICCARDA DONATI, Forese's sister, introduces herself, smiling and ready

Dante meets Piccarda Donati.

to please the pilgrim. The story of her life is well known to Dante; but now she likes to remind him of it. She had commenced to serve God as a nun, and truly was happy in the cloister until, one day, some wicked men, led by one of her own brothers, abducted her from it and forced her into marriage. No, she was not to blame for the sudden interruption of her monastic life; but surely her will was not adamant in the defense of her vows.

"You, who are so fully contented now," Dante inquires, "do you not long for greater happiness in a higher sphere?"

Piccarda's quick reply explains the secret of Paradise. "Brother," she says, "if we longed for a loftier place, our desire would not be in harmony with God's. The nature of this blissful abode is that we all are happy in being one with God's will. 'Tis in his will our very peace abides."

Now Dante knows that Paradise is everywhere—wherever God's infinite grace is felt and man's finite responsiveness obeys.

Piccarda speaks of another soul who, like herself, was to break her vows. Dante looks at CONSTANCE, mother of the Emperor Frederick II, but her radiance does not seem to distract him from his thought.. He is still savoring the meaning and beauty of the words "Tis in his will our very peace abides" when, like a heavy object sinking into deep water, Piccarda fades out of sight, singing 'Ave Maria'.

Once more, Beatrice stresses what she wants her beloved to remember before he climbs to the second sphere —that all the spirits he meets do not dwell where they show themselves but around the throne of the Highest.

CHAPTER TWO

HEAVEN OF MERCURY: THE IMPERIAL VICTORY

Her silence and her face, now newly lit,
commanded me to utter not a word
and yield no more to my inquiring thought.

So, like a dart that of its own accord
reaches its aim before the bow relent,
up to the second realm we quickly soared.

My lady I saw there so radiant,
as soon as in that light she came to dwell,
the planet therefore grew more rutilant.

And if the whole star changed and smiled so well,
imagine what I must have then become,
who was by nature made so changeable.

As in a tranquil, clear aquarium
the fish are drawn to something laid outside,
believing that their meal at last has come,

so I around us countless splendors eyed,
each moving toward us, saying, "Here is one
by whom our love will soon be multiplied."

In the HEAVEN OF MERCURY, where Dante is warmly welcomed by the LOVERS OF EARTHLY FAME, the new blessed souls are vaguely perceived in the luminous halo that encircles them. Like those in the Heaven of the Moon, they, too, seem to remind the beholder of their earthy existence as they appear, one after another, in their recognizable human features. Dante understands that, in the higher spheres, the splendor of God will be so much more dazzling as to make the new spirits visible only to their Creator.

"O happy man, predestined to gaze on the thrones of the Saints before your mortal struggle is done, we are but sparks of the light that fills the heavens; therefore, if you desire to know about us, feel free to raise your questions."

These words are spoken by one of the Spirits. The increasing luster in front of him makes Dante realize that the one who has addressed him is eager to reveal his identity. He also understands that, like Piccarda Donati, this blissful soul is yearning to please him, not out of sheer human friendliness, but only because, being one with God Who is Love, he wishes to share his paradise with him.

Comforted by the affectionate invitation, Dante replies:

"I know that you hide in the light you are shedding; but tell me who you are and why you are showing yourself to me in the Heaven of Mercury."

Now the Spirit resembles the sun that, having vanquished the last remnants of the morning mist, sparkles so clear and fiery it almost hides in its own radiance.

"I am simply JUSTINIAN here, but was known as Emperor on earth," the Spirit says. "It was the Primal Love, the Holy Spirit, who inspired me to start and finish the lofty task of my life. I am the one who reordered the laws for all mankind, removing from their midst what was inadequate and superfluous. So that you may see for yourself how wrong are those who offend the sacred symbol of the law either by using it for their own evil purposes or by openly fighting it, let me tell you the story of the Imperial Eagle."

Dante listens to the story of Rome, from the legend of her birth to the victories of Charlemagne and the dawn of the Holy Roman Empire. But why is Justinian telling Dante all this? Dante already knows it. Oh, but there is something he is learning for the first time. Only now, in the light of God, can he understand what seems so baffling on man's earth—that there is a reason for all the vicissitudes, joyous and sad, which make man's world such as we know it. It is God Who shapes all human events for the ultimate triumph of His Justice. God is Justice; therefore, it is man's duty to cooperate with Him for the advent of order in the world. Why, then, are there so many who, instead of hastening the day of God's Justice on earth, do nothing but prolong disorder and injustice? And why are the few who practice justice and order so lonely and ill-rewarded? Consider, for instance, the case of Romeo of' Villeneuve, the spirit next to Justinian.

ROMEO OF VILLENEUVE, who died fifteen years before Dante was born, did so much for his lord, only to receive as much ill in return. From the day he joined the court of Berengar IV, Count of Provence, he was so zealous and loyal, selfless, and honest, that he succeeded in doubling his lord's renown and riches throughout the land of France. He was even instrumental in finding a royal bridegroom for each of the Count's four daughters. But, one day, envy, the vice of all courts, claimed one more victim.

Accused of mishandling the public treasury, Romeo was too grieved to think of clearing his name. He simply said to the Count that, in all the years of his service, he had made him wealthy and worthy of respect. "Sir, he concluded, "when I came to your court, I had but a horse and a pilgrim's staff. Now give them back to me, and I shall leave in peace." Berengar begged him to stay, but Romeo chose to depart; and only God knows where the old man went and how he struggled till the day of his death.

Dante looks at the light in which the soul of Romeo rests, and cannot help remembering what he had heard about himself in Hell and Purgatory—that he, too, in a few short years, will experience ingratitude and exile.

When Justinian and Romeo are no longer in sight, a doubt preys suddenly on Dante's mind. If the whole history of the Empire, as Justinian said, was governed by Divine Providence for the ultimate realization of its eternal plan, why were the Jews punished for something they had been predestined to do?

Beatrice tells Dante that, if we only look at the human nature of Christ, His death was just inasmuch as it was the result of the same human nature that had sinned; but, if we look at the divine nature of Christ, Son of God, then the injury unjustly suffered by His divinity had to be justly avenged. Dante sees now in a new light not only the fall and destruction of Jerusalem but also man's creation, redemption, and final resurrection.

But why is Beatrice suddenly silent? Her face grows so much brighter, her glance so much more beautiful, that Dante fails to notice that he has already ascended to the loveliness of the next heaven.

CHAPTER THREE

HEAVEN OF VENUS: THE REDEMPTION OF LOVE

As in a flame a single spark is seen,
 and in a voice another voice is heard
when one is still and one fares in between,

so other lights in all that splendor stirred,
and I could see them circling fast or slow
according as God's sight by each is shared.

So fast have the new spirits descended from the Empyrean to meet Dante in the HEAVEN OF VENUS, which represents the degree of their merit, that the swiftest wind coming down from an icy cloud is very slow in comparison.

They all sing 'Hosannah,' and so entrancing is the music of the celestial hymn that Dante is sure he will always long to hear it. They are the SENSUAL LOVERS.

Speaking for all of them, one says to Dante: 'We are so eager to please you that our bliss will not abate if we stay awhile with you."

"Who are you?" asks Dante, encouraged by Beatrice.

"In the same circle, with the same velocity, and with the same thirst for God's light we move together with the Intelligences which influence this Heaven, and which you, a citizen of the earth, described in a poem beginning with the line, 'O Intelligences moving the third heaven."

The Spirit who has spoken is CHARLES MARTEL. In a flash Dante remembers how he had met him barely six years before. Charles Martel, the crowned King of Hungary, visited Florence in the spring of 1294. How young and handsome he was in his regal robe, and how affable and humble, as he passed through the streets of the city, waving to the cheering crowd! He was twenty-three years of age, and therefore no one could ever suspect that he had only a few more months to live. He loved the Florentines, and even mingled and sang with them. On that occasion he expressed his desire to listen to some poetry written not in Latin but in the language of the common people. And so it was that Dante, only six years his senior, was introduced to him. What did His Majesty wish to hear? Anything provided that it was in Tuscan, the glorious language of Florence. Dante read a poem he had just completed, the one which began, "O Intelligences moving the third heaven." At the end of that reading, the king and the poet were friends, for poetry had bound their hearts with the same youthful dream of love and beauty.

"Had I remained a little longer on our earth," Charles Martel continues, still invisible in his blissful light, 'I would have shown you, not with words but with deeds, how good a friend I was to you. In due time, I would have become the ruler of Provence and of Southern Italy if the tyranny of Charles I of Anjou had not provoked the rebellion of the Sicilian people. If my brother Robert could only see, before it is too late, what bitter fruit his evil government will bear!'

"I am grateful to you, my lord," Dante replies, for relating to me what you can read in God. But there is something I fail to comprehend: What makes a sweet seed give birth to a bitter plant? Why must two brothers, reared in the same family, turn out so different one from the other?'

Charles Martel explains to Dante that, in giving each man his own attitude or propensity, the planets act according to God's infinite decree, which aims at the order of the universe and the happiness of mankind, but do not distinguish, in doing so, one home from another. A man is born to be a legislator, another a military leader; one a priest, and another an astronautical architect. Consequently, Esau differs from his brother Jacob. Man should follow his natural inclination, then, to be useful and happy in life. But, unfortunately, one who is born to be a soldier is forced to become a priest, and one who is only good at preaching is crowned a king. God's plan is ever perfect; it is man who often wrecks it and thus destroys himself.

There is sadness in the words of Charles Martel—a sadness that, even in the fulgence of Paradise, keeps Dante aware of the earth to which he must return at the end of his journey.

At this point, another Spirit is willing to speak to Dante, who notices a brighter luminescence in the light next to Charles.

Heartened by Beatrice once again, Dante says: "O blessed Spirit, prove to me that you already know my thoughts, which are reflected in your light."

"Cunizza is my name," the blessed soul begins. "I shine in the Heaven of Venus because it was the influence of this planet that brought me here. No, I am not sorry for the life I led; it is because of my past that I enjoy my present happiness."

CUNIZZA DA ROMANO, Ezzelino's sister, was nearly ninety years old when she died in Florence, in 1280. Dante was then a fifteen-year-old boy. Every Florentine knew Cunizza's story. It seemed nearly impossible that the pious old lady, so generous to the poor, so kind and soft-spoken, had been an altogether different person in her youth. She had had lovers and husbands, and had proved so ready to dispense the beauty of her body that she would have thought it a villainous act to displease anyone who had courteously asked for it, when, one day, the political power of her family having come to an end, and, with it, something else in her heart, she repented of her sins and devoted the rest of her life to God. To God she went back with the same ardor with which she had strayed from Him. And God, Who willingly pardons, pardoned her.

Dante is made to realize that the Spirits who have come down to meet him in the Heaven of Venus are those who happily understood, while still on earth, that only God must claim and cleanse all human love.

The Heaven of the Sun.

CHAPTER FOUR
HEAVEN OF THE SUN: THE TWO BRIGHT GARLANDS

The major minister of nature, bright
dispenser to the world of heaven's worth,
and measurer of time with its own light,

was now my dwelling; but of my ascent
I knew what mortals know of their own thought
before their very thought is evident.

"Thank, oh, thank the Sun of the Angels," Beatrice says to Dante, "for the grace you have been granted of climbing up here."

No human being ever lifted his prayer to God so fast and with such ardent devotion as, prompted by these words, does Dante at this moment. He praises and blesses the Sun of the Angels with such burning faith that even the thought of Beatrice seems suddenly to belong to a long-forgotten past. She cannot help smiling; and it is her smile that calls Dante's attention to a luminous wreath burning like a halo around both of them. It is a large, indescribable garland made up of twelve dazzling suns that look like petals. Dante, who finds himself at the very center of this new splendor, can only think that, if he were still on his earth, he would most likely compare it to the moon in the midst of sailing stars. But he is now in the Heaven of the Sun, and can hardly believe what he hears and sees.

So enrapturing is the song he hears, and so lovely the light he beholds, that he wonders whether it is the light that sings or the song that shines, not knowing which of the two is better—the music or the splendor.

He is still wondering when—look!—the twelve bright suns are seen to move. Three times they circle around him, each time pausing awhile like dancing figures gracefully waiting for the new music to start. Finally, a voice is heard from one of the lights:

Note1) According to the Ptolemaic-Aristotelian cosmology, the sun was a planet rotating around the earth, immobile at the center of the universe. Dante lived nearly three centuries before Copernicus and Galilei.

"You wish to know the name of each flower of this wreath."

Thus, the twelve suns are introduced to Dante.

The first is THOMAS AQUINAS, a theologian and philosopher; the second, ALBERTUS MAGNUS, known as the Universal Doctor; the third, GRATIAN, the founder of the science of Canon Law; the fourth, PETER LOMBARD, the Master of the Sentences; the fifth, SOLOMON, the wisest of all men; the sixth, DIONYSIUS THE AREOPAGITE, the Athenian converted to Christianity by Saint Paul; the seventh, OROSIUS, an historian and apologist of the faith; the eighth, BOETHIUS, a statesman and philosopher of the fifth century; the ninth, ISIDORE OF SEVILLE, a scientist of the early seventh century; the tenth, VENERABLE BEDE, the author of the *Ecclesiastical History of England*; the eleventh, RICHARD OF SAINT VICTOR, a mystical writer of the twelfth century; and the twelfth, SIGIER OF BRABANT, a philosopher, contemporary and rival of Thomas Aquinas.

> Like an alarm clock waking us to know
> God's Bride has risen and now woos her Groom
> with morning prayer so that His love may grow,
>
> for fondly now they call each other home,
> ringing ding-dong with such melodious sound
> that all good souls with love are overcome,
>
> I saw that wheel of glory turn around,
> and answer call to call in such a guise
> and such a sweetness as alone is found
>
> where joy becomes forever paradise.

As soon as the glorious wheel resumes its previous position, and each of the twelve lights returns to its place, Thomas Aquinas tells Dante a story of love and beauty which rings so new that it makes all earthly fables sound like irrelevant and even offensive verbiage. It is the Story of Saint Francis of Assisi, one of the Saints who reveal themselves in the Heaven of the Sun.

FRANCIS OF ASSISI, whom Thomas Aquinas calls Francis of Ascension, was, indeed, like a life-giving sun from the first to the last day of his existence. He was young and strong and burning with love, and yet he chose to marry one whom everyone else despised and abhorred—Lady Poverty herself. He married her for the sake of Christ, and so much he loved her that, inspired by his faith and spurred by his example, others began to follow him, equally in love with his bride, Lady Poverty. And so the Franciscan friars were born—a tiny, peaceful group of men whose only desire was to see and serve Christ in all of His poor, and help the Church against her enemies. But that small company grew, and therefore Francis went to Rome to obtain the blessing of Pope Innocent III on the rigid rule and evangelical work of his "Brothers." Nine years later, in 1223, Pope Honorius III, also, imparted his apostolic benediction on the humble and happy beggars of God. But Francis knew that there were other souls in the world that did not love Christ. So, one day, alone and unarmed, he left for Africa with the intention of preaching the Gospel among the pagans. When he returned to Italy, Christ himself told him how pleased He was with his work. For two years Francis bore the sign of Christ's crucifixion on his hands, until the day Sister Death appeared and took his soul to heaven.

"But why," Thomas Aquinas concludes, "why are the men of God so different from Francis? Why are they no longer in love with Lady Poverty? What madness makes them stray so far from the fold? They do not realize that, by detaching themselves from the spirit of Christ, they will reap nothing but wind and disaster."

Now the wreath of the twelve saints resumes its circular motion like a huge millstone; but before it completes its horizontal gyration, a second wreath appears around the first, so that Beatrice and Dante are now at the center not of one but of two garlands of eternal roses resembling two identical, concentric rainbows in the sky.

With the same inevitable speed with which a magnetic needle points to the north star, Dante turns to the voice that comes out of the first of the twelve petals of the new garland. It is SAINT BONAVENTURE who introduces himself to Dante, and then briefly presents the other singing lights of the farther wreath.

The second is ILLUMINATO, the friar who accompanied Saint Francis to the Holy Land; the third, BROTHER AUSTIN, another disciple of Saint Francis; the fourth, HUGH OF SAINT VICTOR, the teacher of Richard of Saint Victor and Peter Lombard, both mentioned in the inner ring; the fifth, PETER COMESTOR, a biblical scholar of the twelfth century; the sixth, PETER OF SPAIN, the physician and theologian who became Pope John XXI in 1276; the seventh, NATHAN THE PROPHET, the one who fiercely rebuked King David; the eighth, JOHN CHRYSOSTOM, the fourth-century preacher who vehemently reprimanded Emperor Arcadius for the corruption of his court; the ninth, SAINT ANSELM, a theologian who became Bishop of Canterbury in 1093; the tenth, DONATUS, the famous grammarian, teacher of Saint Jerome; the eleventh, RABANUS MAURUS, another theologian, and, finally, JOACHIM OF FLORA, a Calabrian monk whose teachings had been condemned by the Church.

Dante's delight is equal to his astonishment. The phantasmagorical double dance of the Blessed comes to a pause which allows the human pilgrim to breathe and be suddenly aware of doubts in his mind. Is Solomon the wisest of all men or only of kings? And why are Sigier of Brabant and Joachim of Flora, whose earthly teachings so openly clashed with those of the Church, now sharing the same glory with the other Saints?

Thomas Aquinas reminds him of the fact that God is reached in more ways than one, and that all the limitations of the human mind are reconciled in the luminous truth of Paradise. Solomon himself, then, answers a question raised by Beatrice, on Dante's behalf.

"When we resume our bodies," he says, "a greater perfection will be ours insofar as our old unity will be restored; therefore, our radiance will increase."

But Dante's attention seems to be elsewhere. He has just noticed that, when Thomas Aquinas spoke, the heavenly ripple of his words came from the circumference to the center, whereas, now that Beatrice has spoken, the motion of her words goes from the center to the circumference of the circle. He remembers a very simple detail of life en his earth. In a round vase full of water, this moves in circles which grow smaller as they go from the periphery to the center if the vase is struck from the outside; but, if it is struck from the inside, the circles on the water grow larger as they go from the center to the circumference. But why is he still thinking of the earth far away?

When he turns his gaze, a third circle of light appears around the first and the second—another measureless garland of reddish hue.

It is this different color that makes Dante understand that he has been transported to the next planet.

The new wreath does not last. Its myriad lights begin to scatter, half in a vertical, half in a horizontal direction, until they form the shape of a Cross— an indescribable Cross along which, from top to bottom, from arm to arm, new blessed spirits are seen to sparkle like countless specks of dust in a ray of sunlight.

Dante, who has never gazed on anything so beautiful, is all rapt in the vision when a music starts from the Cross and fills the entire planet. The new happiness so overwhelms his senses that not even Beatrice seems to exist any more.

CHAPTER FIVE
HEAVEN OF MARS: THE FIERY CROSS

As through the tranquil and unclouded sky,
from time to time a sudden fire ablaze
shoots down, attracting an unwary eye—

a star, it seems, in quest of some new place,
save that no light is lost where it began,
and its descending is a short-lived race,

so from the extreme right a bright star ran
down to the foot of that majestic Cross
out of the constellation's sparkling span.

Here, in the HEAVEN OF MARS, the WARRIORS OF FAITH appear, reflecting the nature of their earthly merit.

The bright star that has flown to the foot of the Cross has escaped Dante's attention. He is still looking, ecstatic, at its ruddy splendor when he hears this voice:

"Blood of my blood: Whoever but you saw the gates of heaven twice opened?"

Dante looks again and, feeling marvelously at home, is overcome with such bliss that he experiences the sensation of reaching the bottom of grace and paradise. He is in the presence of one of his ancestors, one who loves him, one who has been awaiting him. Were it not so, how could he bear such light?

"My son," the voice continues, "in the great book of God's will I have read of your coming. At last, you have answered my prayer, thanks to the one who made you ready to fly so high. You firmly believe it is God himself Who reveals your thoughts to me; that is why you refrain from asking me who I am and why I am happier than all the others in welcoming you. Yes, you are right; but so that the sacred love, in which I eternally wake, and which makes me athirst with sweet desire, be better fulfilled at this moment, let your undaunted voice express your wish, and I will tell you all that I have been yearning to tell."

Looking at Beatrice, who reassures him, Dante replies:

"Being mortal still, I am unable to express my gratitude for your paternal joy, but tell me who you are, who adorn this lively jewel with your light."

At this point, beaming with pride, CACCIAGUIDA, Dante's great-great-grandfather, tells the story of his life as if he were still in Florence. Or is it, rather, the story of ancient Florence itself?

"Once upon a time, my son, our city lay safe within her walls, and sobriety and modesty were considered virtues by all her inhabitants. In the good old days, women did not go around ostentatiously dressed, wearing, that is, garments more precious and richer than themselves. When a baby girl was born, her father was happy, and was not frightened by the thought of a dowry. No such thing as birth control was practiced then, and married life was not a secret school of turpitude and lust. With my very eyes I saw a nobleman called Bellincion Berti walk through the streets in a humble cloak without ornaments of silver or gold. And his gentle wife never wore any lipstick or powder on her face. They were modest and simple, those women of my time. They took care of their homes, happy to watch over a cradle. They told beautiful tales to their children, who gathered around them and listened to the sweet music of their native tongue. Today, instead, things are not the same. Florence is no longer the city she used to be. I was born to a different society, believe me, my son. I was a soldier, and fought for the Cross in the Second Crusade. Conrad III, Emperor of Swabia, knighted me, so much I pleased him with my service. Fighting for the Cross of Christ, I died, and climbed from my martyrdom to this peace.'

Dante is so proud of his great-great-grandfather, a martyr of the faith, that, for a moment, he even rejoices over the detail of his own derived nobility.

"Sir," he says, with respect and love, "you have made me so happy that I feel like a different person. But oh, tell me more about the good old days of our Florence."

Cacciaguida's light grows suddenly more beautiful, like coals revived by a blowing wind. His voice becomes so much more tender and paternal that it makes Dante wish it would last forever. So Dante learns from the very lips of his glorious ancestor not only the names of the most important families of ancient Florence but also what causes her present political chaos.

"Father, dear father," Dante asks at the end of his long reminiscing, is it true that fate has so much grief in store for me? During my journey through Hell and Purgatory, while I was with Virgil, I heard sad things about my future. Though I am not afraid to face what I must, yet I am somewhat perturbed. Tell me, I beg you, what I should know, for, if expected, anguish strikes less hard."

Once more Dante hears about his impending exile and his sorrowful years ahead. He will be banished from Florence, and will have to abandon what he cherishes most. He will beg for his daily bread, and know the humiliation of climbing more than once the stairs of a home not his own.

"Father," Dante says, "if I am destined to lose my native land, I hope I will not lose my few remaining friends with the truth of my poem."

"Naturally," Cacciaguida replies to him, "all those who have a guilty conscience will hate you for what you write; but do not let their resentment stop you. Just let them scratch where they feel the itch. At first, they will shun your truthful voice, but then they will benefit from it. Remember: the stronger the wind, the higher peaks it strikes. That is why you have been granted to see the souls of the sorrowful valley, and of the mountain, and now, at last, these glorious heavens of God. Indeed, a great honor, my son."

Beatrice detects some sadness in Dante's eyes. "Look!" she says, "Look over there!'

Invited by Cacciaguida, eight new spirits detach themselves from the radiant Cross and reveal their names to Dante. Among these warrior-saints are Charlemagne, Roland, and Godfrey, the leader of the First Crusade.

Now that Dante turns to Beatrice to learn from her gaze what she wants him to do, her face is so luminous that he understands, once again, that a higher heaven has been reached.

The Heaven of Mars.

CHAPTER SIX

HEAVEN OF JUPITER: THE 'M' AND THE EAGLE

As, judging by the greater happiness
that he derives from his good deeds, a man
can tell the progress of his virtuousness,

so, when I saw her wondrous splendor grown,
I knew that the gyration of the sphere
was ampler now, together with my own.

Here, in the HEAVEN OP JUPITER, where the JUST RULERS appear,
Dante sees the most impressive spectacle so far. The blessed souls that come
to meet him in this Jovial planet remind him of birds that, having quenched
their thirst in a rill, resume their flight in such a varied formation as to resemble
several letters of the alphabet.

Dante stares, entranced, at the sparkling lights flying and singing around
him. They form now a *D*, now an *L*, and, as each new letter is formed, they
pause awhile and briefly end their song as if eager to gaze upon the glowing
majesty of their concerted effort. Thus new vowels and consonants appear in
the immensity of the planet, like iridescent fireworks spreading in every direction
and gaining in beauty. But, unlike fireworks, these lights do not fizzle and die:
they grow larger and more lasting as they weave a tapestry of wonderment
from one to the other extremity of the heavenly sphere.

Dante, who looks more attentively, finally reads a full sentence written in
light by the blessed spirits in their final arrangement: DILIGITE IUSTITIAM
QUI IUDICATIS TERRAM, which means: "Love justice, you who judge the
earth."

No sooner has Dante read the solemn Latin phrase than each of the five
words begins to disintegrate and crumble, like a cascade of incandescent fire, in
the same direction. The lights of each letter, flying and falling, convene at last,
brighter and lovelier, in the conclusive gothic *M* of the sentence. Meanwhile, the
entire Heaven of Jupiter looks like a disk of silver with edges of burning gold.

From the hollow of the massive capital *M*, the only letter left, countless
lights are seen to rise, each less or more tall according to the power granted by
the Sun that sets them on fire with his love. When all these lights rest in their
pre-established place, the top of the *M* takes on the shape of the head and
neck of an Eagle.

Like a flash, this thought runs through Dante's mind: Could it be God himself painting at this very moment one of His heavens?

Joyously obeying the Mind of God, the blessed Spirits do the rest. They place themselves in such a way that, first, they transform the down-strokes of the *M* into what resembles a lily-pattern; then, with a slight motion, they shape the wings and full body of the Eagle. Thus, the Eagle of Justice appears in all its immortal majesty.

Dante can hardly believe his own eyes, and, were he not sure of being in Heaven, where, as Beatrice has repeatedly told him, only Truth exists, he would perhaps be tempted by doubt. He understands the significance of the Eagle. He knows what God expects of those who rule the earth—Justice and nothing but Justice. But why has the Eagle been formed out of the letter M, instead of another? Could it be that, when God's Justice triumphs on man's earth, a peaceful Millennium will finally begin? Or does the *M* mean Mind-of-God, that is, eternal Justice?

Enchanted by the vision of the living Eagle, Dante is none the less aware of what has made it possible. Each of the souls resembles a ruby in which the reflection of the sun is so bright as to create the impression that the sun itself is sparkling there.

Finally, the beak of the Eagle opens, and such song comes out that Dante fails to compare it to anything he might have heard. It is the hymn of Justice, sung in unison by all the Just Rulers. So united are they in Divine Justice that the 'I' and "Mine", which Dante hears, can only mean "We" and "Ours."

"O everlasting flowers of eternal bliss," Dante exclaims, emboldened, "tell me, I beg you, what no one on earth has ever been able to tell me. If a man is just, but has never heard of Christ, is he excluded from Heaven?'"

The Eagle of Justice reassures him. Man's limited intellect cannot fathom the will of God. If God is Justice, and all human justice is a pale reflection thereof, why should He condemn a man who is naturally just? Therefore, blessed those who practice Justice on earth, even though they have not been directly enlightened by the living Word. But woe to the just rulers of the world who should know better than oppress their subjects with their wicked demands!

Another hymn resounds in the Heaven of Jupiter; then a murmuring rises up the neck of the Eagle, and a new word comes forth.

Dante is told to look closely at the light that makes the pupil of the Eagle, and at the five others that form its eyebrow. The first is introduced as DAVID; the other four are TRAJAN, CONSTANTINE, WILLIAM II OF SICILY, and RHIPEUS THE TROJAN.

Obviously, Dante has not fully comprehended the meaning of divine Justice as yet or he would not ask why Trajan and Rhipeus, two pagans, are together with prophets like David and Hezekiah.

The Eagle replies that Emperor Trajan and the Trojan Rhipeus were so just in a world of injustice that, although pagan, they were rewarded by God with a glimpse of His direct revelation; that is why they are now in Paradise together with David and Hezekiah.

As a skylark first sings in the sun, and then is silent, happily basking in the sweet echo of its own melody, so now the Eagle refrains from speaking, to savor the pleasure of its own music.

Dante looks at his beloved guide; but, this time, Beatrice does not smile lest the greater light of her eyes should turn him into a heap of ashes.

The two have climbed to the Heaven of Saturn where the radiant smile of Beatrice, if not partly veiled, would surely kill Dante as lightning kills a tree.

CHAPTER SEVEN
HEAVEN OF SATURN: THE GOLDEN LADDER

"Let your attention follow now your eyes,
and let your eyes be mirrors to the show
that in this heaven right before you lies."

Dante is so happy to do as Beatrice commands that the pleasure of obeying her wish equals the ecstasy he experiences on finding himself in the HEAVEN OF SATURN. Here he is about to meet the CONTEMPLATIVE SPIRITS.

Contemplation! It is this very word that makes him look at the new planet wheeling around him silently, without the music, that is, which has heretofore been heard in the six lower heavens. It shines like a flawless crystal with a golden conflagration in its center. It is this central fire that suddenly attracts Dante's attention.

It is a golden ladder rising so high that Dante cannot even surmise where it might end. Its top is concealed in the light, innumerable miles away. Only its rungs can be seen, made up of countless Spirits, so luminous and glad that it seems that the light of all the stars has decided to shine in this one place alone. Like birds that stir in the nest at dawn, or like others flying no more to return, these blessed souls sparkle along the Golden Ladder, some moving toward its bottom, some shining with a circular motion. At a certain rung of the Ladder they all pause; then, all at once, they separate, forming several groups. Some climb, some stay, and some direct themselves toward Dante. One light draws so near that Dante is sure he will soon know whose soul hides in it. Instead, the Spirit remains silent.

"I know it is love you are showing me," Dante says to the light in front of him, "but, though I do not deserve your answer, in the name of Beatrice I beg you to tell me why you, only you, have come so close to me, and why no sweet music rings in this sphere."

"It is," the Spirit answers, "because, being still a mortal man, you have such weak, defective hearing that, if you could heed our song, you would instantly be overwhelmed by it. For the same reason Beatrice has refrained from smiling. As to your first question, I want you to know that I have been chosen to speak to you not because I am worthier than the others but only because each of us here freely fulfills the tasks assigned by the Providence that governs the world. Look at the lights on the rungs of the Ladder. They all are burning with desire to please and welcome you."

Dante is still far from understanding this gentle reply of the blessed soul. He cannot even guess why, of so many thousands of Spirits, this one in particular has been predestined by God to welcome him in their name. Yet how he hopes to understand, once and for all, the word that has always disconcerted his mind—Predestination.

Affectionately, the Spirit explains:

"Oh, no! Not even the soul of the angel closest to God can answer your question. What you ask delves so deeply into the eternal decree that no created intelligence can ever fathom it. Therefore, when you go back, tell the whole mortal world not to presume to scan the abysses of God's immortal counsel. The human mind, which here is enlightened by His splendor, is merely a whiff of smoke upon your earth."

"But who are you?" Dante asks humbly, embarrassed.

SAINT PETER DAMIAN reveals his identity. and briefly tells the story of his life. He was a poor sinner until, by the grace of God, he realized how futile and empty all human honors are. It was then he left the world and started his true existence in a monastery. There, he fell so deeply in love with contemplative life, through which he could soar to God while still in the misery of his flesh, that, when he was made a Cardinal, once more he preferred the obscurity of his hermitage to the pomp and luxury of public renown.

"But now," Peter Damian concludes, "the monastery is no longer the refuge of the soul. It has become a nest of vanity, a harbor of mundanity and pride, a flagrant example of shame. O patient God, till when will you bear all this?"

These last words reverberate like a thunderbolt through the planet. All the souls converge around Peter Damian, echoing his invective against the degeneracy of monastic regulations.

For the first time in Paradise, Dante is afraid, and, as the entire Heaven of Saturn quavers as if in terror, he turns to Beatrice, frantic, and with sudden anguish in his gaze.

Beatrice comforts him as a loving mother would comfort a child frightened by a nightmare. She reads all his thoughts, and therefore knows what is vexing his mind at this moment. He thinks that this cry of indignation, still spreading through the sphere of Saturn, has hurled him back on the earth and the reality of its anger.

"Why are you so perturbed?" she tells him. "Don't you know that you are in Heaven, where everything we do is motivated by holy zeal? If an outburst of just indignation has shaken you so, what would have happened if you could have seen my smile and heard the song of these Contemplative Spirits? Now turn, and look at something new."

Dante turns, and sees hundreds of souls, each resembling a small, luminous sphere. They are beautiful, but their beauty is ineffably enhanced by the rays that one exchanges with the other.

The first and largest of the new lights advances toward Dante, and urges him to raise whatever question he wishes to ask. "If you knew, as I know, the fire of charity burning within us, you would have manifested all of your thoughts already. But since you are still hesitant to ask, I want to speak to you first."

Thus, SAINT BENEDICT tells Dante how, one day long ago, he founded his monastic Order at Monte Cassino. There, following in his footsteps, his disciples prayed and worked ('Ora et Labora' was their only rule) and thus brought souls to God.

"But today," he continues, "the walls of the abbey, once a harbor of virtue and sanctity, have become a den of wicked, covetous men who, for love of money, even sell the things of God and His Church. These unworthy monks have forgotten the Apostle Peter, who started his mission without any gold; have forgotten Francis of Assisi, who wanted the example of his humility to guide his friars; and have forgotten me, who only believed in prayer and work. Alas, what black results from such white beginnings."

Dante expects another explosion of heavenly zeal after this new condemnation of degenerate monks and friars. Saint Benedict, instead, concludes his talk with an act of faith in God's unfailing assistance.

At this point, all the Spirits begin to climb on the Golden Ladder, disappearing into the brightness overhead.

"You too," Beatrice says to Dante. "You are so close to the face of God that your gaze had better be sharp and free of all earthly recollections. For the last time, then, look down at that speck of dust far away."

Dante sees the seven planets in all their rotating immensity, and then, nearly invisible beneath the last of them, a small, insignificant speck—the earth.

"The flower-bed that makes wild beasts of us!" he sighs, looking at it with a sense of relief as if he were never to be part of its horror again.

CHAPTER EIGHT

HEAVEN OF THE FIXED STARS: THE TRIUMPH OF CHRIST

As, having rested near her fledglings' nest
during the night that darkens everything,
a bird reclimbs her leafy branch, in quest

of dear, familiar light, and food to bring
to famished, open beaks—wherefore she dreads
no grievousness of labor and no sting:

perched on the tallest twig, she fondly waits,
anticipating time, the rising sun,
fixedly looking for the dawn to break:

so was my lady standing in attention,
turned to that region where, less quick to run,
the sun is almost resting with intention.

Beatrice is waiting for the new wonder to break. Now that even the sun lies far below, what will the face of God be like? The seven planets are underneath, and all their combined splendor is nothing but a shadow of the light about to rise.

Looking at her, Dante waits, uttering no word. It is she who, always aware of his thoughts and feelings, finally points out to him the beginning of the new glory.

"Here is the Triumph of Christ," she says, "and here, the purpose of every rotating sphere."

Dante turns to Beatrice.

"Do not worry!" she reassures him. "No mortal eye can gaze upon such light. This is the wisdom and power that opened a path between God and man."

Having caught but a glimpse of the human figure of Christ, Dante turns to Beatrice again and, for the first time, is able to see the full splendor of her smile.

"Yes, look, look at me," she says, "for you have seen so much already that you are strong enough to see me as I am."

Dante is so happy that he feels he has always known her in the fullness of her radiance. The story of his past is so faint, so vague, that it looks like the forgotten page of a book read long, long ago.

"If my face makes you so jubilant," Beatrice says, "look at that blessed garden enlivened by the rays of Christ. The Apostles and Mary are there."

Like sunrays suddenly showering out of a broken cloud, the Apostles and the Blessed Mother appear. So bright, so beautiful, so much more dazzling than all of them is the Virgin Mary that Dante does not even know how to praise or pray.

> The sweetest-sounding melodies of earth
> that to his utmost bliss man hears enrapt
> are like rent clouds that give to thunder birth,
>
> compared to the true music of that lyre
> which crowned the lovely sapphire all about
> wherewith the clearest sphere is all on fire.

The triumph of Christ has become the triumph of Mary, His mother, for an Angel comes down from the magnificence of all that light, and begins to circle around her, weaving a sparkling crown all about her.

"O Queen of Heaven," the Angel says, singing, "I have come to escort you to the highest sphere which, as you return with your Son, will become brighter for your glow."

At these angelic words, all the blessed spirits fondly outstretch their arms toward Mary like children clamoring to be caressed and embraced by their mother. Then, oblivious of all else, they begin to sing, "O Queen of Heaven," with such tenderness and love that Dante, too, forgets whatever is not an echo of that song.

Preceded by the Apostles, the blessed Mother is soon to return to the Empyrean where God abides in all His glory.

Dante hopes to see the majestic procession, and wonders what will happen now that he is so close to the face of God. Will he be able to sustain His light? Will Mary notice him at all? Will Beatrice fail to help him? Will he talk to the Apostles?

These and other questions flash through his mind as the last echo of the song still rings in his heart.

CHAPTER NINE
THE TRIPLE EXAMINATION: FAITH, HOPE, AND CHARITY

O Brotherhood, elected to partake
of God's meek Lamb, Who fully sates you all
and yet your hunger never seems to break,

let one small crumb down from your table fall
so that by grace this man your Supper taste
before death comes between him and his call!

Dante stares at the new Blessed Spirits, and easily understands why each of them resembles a fiery comet with a blazing tail: they are so happy in their eternal delight that they cannot hide their inner bliss. But it is their dance that makes him think of the wheels of a clock. According to the degree of their earthly merit, these Saints move about in their glow, one faster, one slower, one larger, one smaller, just like the wheels inside a clock, the slowest of which seems not to move at all.

From the brightest of these lights a fire descends, and circles Beatrice three times as if to tell her that her prayer has been heard. Dante will soon partake of their bliss.

Beatrice is so grateful to the soul that has silently answered her question that, to show her delight, she says:

"Dear SAINT PETER, glorious Apostle to whom our Lord entrusted the keys of His Kingdom, examine this man on faith—on that faith that enabled you to walk on the sea."

There is no time to waste. Instead of panicking at the thought that none other than Saint Peter is about to examine him on the difficult subject of faith, Dante trusts Beatrice implicitly. Would she have thought of this if she believed him incapable of answering?

Like a student quickly reviewing his notes a few moments before the test, Dante thinks of the first question he may be asked, and mentally repeats the answer he will give.

"Say, good Christian," Saint Peter begins. "What is Faith?"

Dante looks at Beatrice for reassurance. She smiles, as if to tell him, "I know you know the answer."

"Faith," Dante replies, "is the substance of things we hope for, and the evidence of things we fail to see. This is how Saint Paul, a dear friend of yours, defined it."

"You are right," Saint Peter agrees; "but why did my friend mention first the substance and then the evidence?"

"The profound mysteries which I see so clearly up here, and which, on earth, are so incomprehensible that I can do nothing but believe, are the substance. The evidence, instead, is all that we base our belief on."

"Well said," Saint Peter agrees. "You know all about this coin. But tell me now: Do you have it in your purse?"

"Oh, yes, yes, I have it. I believe so firmly that I have no doubt whatsoever about my faith."

"But how did you happen to have it? Why do you believe?"

"Because the inspiration of the Holy Spirit, which fills both the Old and the New Testament, is so great a proof that all my words are nothing, compared to it."

"Yes, but how can you say that the Old and the New Testament were inspired by the Holy Spirit?"

"Because of the miracles that followed."

"But why were they miracles?"

"The very fact that you, a poor, unlearned man, could bring the world to Christ is a miracle that, alone, would make me believe."

The whole heavenly court is so pleased with Dante's answer that their song resounds in the air; but Saint Peter wants to hear more.

"God has assisted you well," he continues; "but tell me now all the things in which you believe."

"I believe in one God, one and eternal, Who moves all heavens with love and desire... And I believe in three Eternal Persons, so much one and so much three that they can say 'I am' as well as 'We are'. This is the beginning; this is the spark that lights up this lively fire burning in my heart like a star in the sky."

Saint Peter embraces Dante three times, blessing him for his delightful reply.

SAINT JAMES appears at this point, and Beatrice asks him to examine Dante on Hope.

"Do not be afraid, my son," Saint James reassures him.

"Instead, lift up your eyes! He who comes here from the mortal world can bear the power of our light."

Dante is ready for his second examination.

"Since you have been granted to see God before your death, Saint James begins, "tell me three things: What is Hope? To what extent does it adorn your mind? And how did you come to possess it?"

Beatrice speeds to Dante's rescue.

"I can assure you," she says to Saint James, "that in the whole Church Militant no one has in his heart a greater hope than this man. That is why he has been granted the grace of coming, still alive, from his Egypt to our Jerusalem. Therefore, let him answer only the second and third of your questions."

"Hope," Dante replies, "is a firm expectation of future glory, caused by God's grace and strengthened by our own merit. It is a light that comes to me from many sources; but David is the one who instilled it in my heart with his *Psalms* and then you with your *Epistle*. Hope is so abundant in me that I long to share it with others."

Saint James is pleased with the answer, but he wishes to hear more from such a good student.

"What does Hope promise you?" he asks.

"It promises me," Dante replies promptly, "what Isaiah calls the double light of those who share God's friendship—the light of soul and body, that is. And it promises me what your own brother, John, described with greater accuracy in his *Apocalypse*—the glory of the snow-white Stoles."

Once more, the heavenly Court resounds with a song of approval.

Will the third examination be as easy as the first two? Dante is not sure. He only knows that there will be a third examination, for, after all, what is Faith, or Hope, without Charity?

The third splendor appears right between the first and the second—it is SAINT JOHN who has come to take his place between Saint Peter and Saint James.

Like one who sharpens his gaze to see a partial eclipse of the sun, and, in doing so, is dazzled blind by its excessive radiance, Dante tries to look upon the new light in front of him, only to be struck by its supernatural might.

He turns to Beatrice but—where is she? He cannot see her. He is blind. What will happen now? How will he be able to see the face of God? Oh, where is Beatrice? If she is still next to him, why can't he see her? He is blind! He is blind."

"Do not be alarmed," Saint John quickly comforts him. "The one who leads you has the power to restore your sight with her healing gaze. But before that happens, I want your reason to compensate for the temporary loss of your vision. Tell me then: What is Charity?"

"Charity," Dante replies, "is the Supreme Good that gladdens this heavenly Court; it is the Alpha and Omega, the beginning and end of all things, great and small, which Love teaches me to cherish. It is God himself."

"Explain what you just said," Saint John comments. "Who made your charity aim so high?"

"Once we learn that something is good," Dante hastens to answer, "the greater its perfection, the more we are drawn to it. Therefore, God being the Supreme and perfect Good, in him alone can we find our ultimate bliss. This truth I have learned not only from Plato but even from you, who wrote that Love is the greatest of all commandments."

"And from no one else?"

"Oh, yes: from all those things that make our hearts turn lovingly to God—the existence of the world and of man, the sacrifice of Christ for the sake of my life, and the promise of eternal happiness to those who hope as I do: all this has taught me true love. And something else—the fact that I was commanded to love my neighbor as much as I love myself."

"Holy, Holy, Holy." is the new hymn of rejoicing sung by the heavenly Court.

Dante's sight is suddenly restored, whereupon he is able to recognize the healing gaze of Beatrice and the undiminished splendor of Peter, James, and John. He can see! He can see!

As he looks around like one who awakens in a familiar room, he detects a fourth light right above him.

"He is ADAM," Beatrice explains, "the first man created by God."

Dante is so jubilant, now that he has passed his three examinations and his vision has been restored, that he becomes rather inquisitive and garrulous. He wants to know from Adam, the first of all men, things that no one on earth was ever able to ask of him: How long he stayed in the Garden of Eden, how old he was when he died, and what language he spoke.

Adam answers all these questions, happy to please our earthly pilgrim.

"Glory be to the Father, and to the Son, and to the Holy Spirit," all the Saints now sing in unison. What Dante hears and sees is like the brilliant laughter of the universe. Oh, joy, Oh ineffable gladness! Oh, life full of love and peace. Oh, wealth that breeds no greed!

At the conclusion of the hymn, the light of Saint Peter begins to grow red and livelier, and its new color seems to eclipse the whiteness of the others. There is sudden silence now in heaven.

"If I change color," Saint Peter says to Dante, "do not be afraid. It is because the one who on earth usurps my place— my place, my place—has made of my tomb a stinking cesspool of blood. As far as we in Heaven are concerned, the Holy See is vacant, for, instead of the Vicar of Christ, Satan now rules in Rome."

At these words, all the Saints, including Beatrice, blush. The entire heaven shows the flaming color of indignation and shame.

Dante is not frightened by the unexpected discoloring of all the lights, for he remembers that it is zeal, and zeal alone, that motivates all things in Heaven. He looks at the red conflagration around him, and thinks of what must have happened to the sun and the stars at the moment of Christ's death on the hill of Calvary.

Saint Peter's voice is heard again, and Dante can hardly recognize it.

"The Church of Christ," the Apostle continues, "was not reared with my blood so that my successors might sell it for gold, but only for the gain of eternal happiness in heaven. It was not our intention that the Pope should favor a party instead of another, and that the keys I received from Our Lord should be used to obtain false privileges and benefits. How well we can see from up here those ravenous wolves disguised as shepherds... But God, I am sure, will come to our aid to save the glory of Rome once more. Now you, my son, when you return to your earth, speak up, and tell the whole world what you have heard and seen."

Dante's attention is attracted by sparks falling down and glistening like numberless flakes of snow: it means that all the blessed spirits are ready to start their flight to the Empyrean, and that he, Dante, is closer to the face of God.

"Look down for the last time," Beatrice tells him. Dante looks down on the earth once more, and cannot believe that he ever lived in such a puny, petty speck of dust— the flower-bed that makes wild beasts of us. So he turns his gaze on Beatrice again, only to find it much more ravishing, much more indescribable than ever. Now he knows that, together with all the blessed Spirits, he is already in the Primum Mobile, which precedes the Empyrean.

Dante's Triple Examination.

CHAPTER TEN
PRIMUM MOBILE: THE LUMINOUS POINT

In the PRIMUM MOBILE, as soon as he looks at Beatrice, and succeeds in gazing into her eyes, Dante sees a luminous point reflected in them, so dazzling that it causes him to look elsewhere for an instant. When he looks at it again, he sees it so distant and small that, compared to it, the tiniest star we see would look as big as a moon. Yet, despite its immeasurable distance, the dazzling point clearly shows nine rings rotating around it like wheels of fire, the first of which, being closer to the center, is the fastest and brightest.

Beatrice smiles, and tells Dante what it is that he has just seen reflected in her eyes. The point is the Image of God, and its nine rings are the nine Orders of Angels.

Dante understands that that point and those rings are like the ideal projection of the order of the universe. Why, then, do the earth and the planets not follow the same disposition as revealed by that point and those circles?

Beatrice explains that, indeed, the divine model is perfectly and harmoniously followed by the sensible world; one must only remember that, the greater the virtue which God assigns, the greater is its influence, whether or not we see it with our human, imperfect vision. Every heaven, therefore, is to be measured not according to its apparent size but according to the Intelligence that influences it.

At the word "Intelligence," all the Angels—the Intelligences of the heavens, that is—reveal themselves to Dante like sparks rising from molten metal, each forming a conflagration of its own.

How many Angels are there?

Dante is told by Beatrice that they surpass in number every multitude of earthly things. In other words, they are more than all the leaves or all the drops of water or all the grains of sand put together.

At this point, all the nine angelic hierarchies, divided into three groups, are introduced to Dante in all their blazing glory. They are, in the order of their proximity to God, and, consequently, of their brilliance, SERAPHIM, CHERUBIM, THRONES; DOMINIONS, VIRTUES, POWERS; and PRINCIPALITIES, ARCHANGELS, ANGELS.

But why is Beatrice silent and almost unmindful of the concerted music ringing throughout the Primum Mobile? She is so absorbed in herself that Dante wonders if she is still aware of him.

"In that luminous point which you have seen reflected in my eyes awhile ago—in God himself—I have read what you long to know. In Him, as in one point, converge all place and time." And now Beatrice tells Dante what no false preacher or prophet on earth can ever know. She tells him about the creation of Angels, the first rebellion in heaven, the difference between human and angelic intelligence, and such other things as can only be read in the indivisible, infinite, omniscient light of God.

The Empyrean.

CHAPTER ELEVEN

THE EMPYREAN: THE RIVER, THE ROSE AND THE BEES

Splendor of intellect, with love replete;
Love of the one true good full of delight;
Delight that far transcends what you call sweet.

Beyond the largest of the material heavens—that is, past the Primum Mobile—Beatrice grows so radiant that Dante decides not to try to describe her beauty any more. Her beauty, he says, so transcends his comprehension that only God, Who made it, can fully enjoy it. Yet he keeps looking at her, basking in all her light, and totally oblivious to all else until she speaks to him.

"We have left the Primum Mobile, and are now in the EMPYREAN, the heaven of pure light. Here you will see the Angels as they really are. and the Saints as they will be on Judgment Day.'

Dante notices that there is no motion in this heaven of pure light.

"It is," Beatrice explains, "because God's love, which satisfies this sphere so completely as to make it immobile, welcomes right here those who must make themselves ready for the utmost fruition of His light."

The Empyrean, then, is the real, eternal abode of the Angels and Saints, and it is from this place that they have come down, as mere reflections, to meet and welcome Dante and Beatrice in the various heavens below. Oh, if they were so dazzling there, what must they be like up here, in their permanent home? And how close are they to God?

Dante is rapt in these thoughts when a river of light is seen, flowing down between two banks painted with eternal springtime. Countless lively sparks leap out of the river, fly straight to the flowers that bloom on each side, and conceal themselves in their colored petals, sipping all their fragrance. Finally, inebriated, they speed back and plunge into the wondrous whirls of the river. Some are going. some are coming, as in a childlike contest of light and scent, of scent and light.

What is the meaning of this?

"It pleases me to see," Beatrice says, "that you are burning to know what this is all about. But only if you drink of this water will you be able to quench your thirst. For the time being, this I can tell you—that the river, the countless sparks that leap up and return, and the laughter of the grass are but a pre-announcement of the truth they conceal. Not that these things are deficient in themselves; it is your faulty vision that prevents you from seeing more."

As an infant that, having waited longer than usual for its mother's milk, runs with its greedy glance to her breast, so Dante kneels on the bank of the river, eager to drink of its glistening water. Suddenly, as soon as his eyelashes touch the waves, what looked like a river a moment ago appears to be now a circular figure, a splendid globe. Like people who instantly remove their masks and thus reveal their true identity, all the sparks and blossoms around Dante become the two courts of heaven— Angels and Saints in all their bliss.

But how can Dante describe the splendid globe before him?

Its circumference would be too big a belt for the sun, and its light, as far as it extends, is the reflection of but one ray coming directly from God.

Dante can only think of a lake at the bottom of a hill, in which the hill itself can proudly mirror the many-colored beauty of its new spring. All the Saints, in fact, group upon group, tier upon tier, seem to mirror themselves in the shining globe underneath them. They form a measureless Rose stretching with all its petals beyond the limits of human imagination. But, instead of losing itself in its quest, Dante's vision absorbs the whole beauty of this celestial flower, for, here in the Empyrean, which is beyond space, God rules directly, without the intermediary laws of nature, and, therefore, without the concept of proximity or distance.

"Look!" Beatrice says to Dante. "Look how large is the number of the snow-white Stoles! Look how far our City extends!"

Dante looks at all the glorious Thrones of the Blessed, arranged through the various petals of the MYSTICAL ROSE, and notices an empty seat among them.

"That seat is waiting," Beatrice explains, "for the noble soul of Henry VII of Luxembourg."

Dante seems to pay no attention to Beatrice for something new has come to entrance and baffle his eyes.

He sees all the Angels like a murmuring swarm of bees coming down and flying around the white Rose. Their faces are fiery-red, their wings are golden, and their garments so white that the whitest snow is black in comparison. The heavenly bees circle the Rose and, going from petal to petal, transmit to all the Saints the warmth of their love and the ecstasy of their peace. Their number is so large that they hide the whole wide Rose beneath the gold of their fluttering wings; and yet, dazed as he is, Dante can still behold each petal and each bee, for nothing can interfere between his glance and God's very light.

How many times do the Angels come and go? Are those the same Angels, or new and different ones, who, each new moment (if we can still think in terms of time), take a new sip of God's inexhaustible love and hasten to bring it down to the Blessed?

Dante cannot tell. He can only compare himself—but what a feeble comparison this is—to a barbarian who sees the grandeur of Rome for the first time, or to one who, upon crossing the threshold of Saint Peter's, looks, ecstatic, at the glaring majesty of its dome and is even afraid of moving one step further.

In a stupor, Dante turns to Beatrice to tell her that he has finally understood the general form and structure of Paradise, but Beatrice is no longer at his side. There is, instead, an old, venerable, kindly man who smiles at Dante like an affectionate father.

"Where is she?" Dante asks.

"Beatrice sent me here," the old man answers, "so that your wish may be fulfilled. She is there—look!—in her throne of bliss in the third tier from the top."

Dante sees Beatrice, seated in her place of glory, so high in the Rose that the distance between the bottom of the ocean and the region of clouds and thunder is nothing but a short, easy step.

"Beatrice! Beatrice!" Dante says, joining his hands in prayer. "You have descended to hell to save me from death. You have brought me from evil to virtue, from servitude to freedom, from darkness to light. To you alone I owe the beauty and grace of all that I have seen and heard. Therefore, so that my soul may remain as pure as you have made it, oh, let me die now, in the midst of this heavenly triumph."

Beatrice smiles from her throne.

SAINT BERNARD, the old man, introduces himself to Dante, and urges him to uplift his eyes toward the highest throne in the Rose. "The Queen of Heaven is there," he adds.

Dante looks up, and sees the Blesses Mother surrounded by thousands of Angels, each different from the other in intensity of splendor and joyousness of flight. In their midst, Mary is so beautiful that her beauty reaches the eyes of every Saint and makes them glow.

At this point, even if he had a vocabulary as rich as his imagination, Dante would not attempt to describe the happiness of the Virgin Mary, so close to God, her Son.

When Dante looks at her again, he sees an Angel kneeling in her presence, and hears, intoned by the same Angel, the hymn "Hail, Mary, full of grace," the rest of which is sung by the entire heavenly Court with such devotion and ardor as make the whole Rose the brighter for it.

"Holy father," Dante implores, "you who have left your happy throne to be here at my side, tell me, I beg you, the name of that Angel, up there, who alone can look into the eyes of our Holy Queen, and seems so deeply in love that his face is all on fire."

"He is the Archangel Gabriel," Saint Bernard replies, "who conveyed to Mary the joyous tidings of God's Incarnation. But now behold the Blessed Seniors of this Court. Saint Bernard singles out Adam, Saint Peter, Saint John the Evangelist, Moses, Saint John the Baptist, Saint Lucy, and then apologizes for not mentioning the others.

"Your time is running short, my son," the holy man says. "Come then, and let me see what I can do for you. Now that you are close to the face of God, only one person can help you—our Blessed Mother. Come."

The prayer to the Madonna.

CHAPTER TWELVE
THE ONE AND THREE

Virgin and mother, daughter of your son,
humble and high far more than creature born,
predestined goal of an eternal plan,

You are the one who rendered human nature
so noble that its maker proudly chose
to be His own creation's very creature.

Love—it was love was kindled in your womb,
whose very warmth in the eternal peace
made this our blossom germinate and bloom.

You are amongst us here a noonday sun
of charity, and to mortal men down there
a font of hope you are—a lively one.

Lady, so great are you, of worth so high,
that he who longs for grace and asks not you
forces his longing on no wings to fly.

Not only does your kindness succor those
who ask, but freely many a time it comes
and far ahead of all their asking goes.

In you is mercy, pity is in you,
magnificence in you, and in you dwells
whatever goodness in mankind is true.

"You alone, O Blessed Mother," Saint Bernard concludes, "you alone can grant this mortal man such virtue as will enable him to gaze upon God, his ultimate salvation. Come to his aid, Holy Queen. Beatrice and all the Saints are praying for him along with me."

Yes, Beatrice and all the Saints, their hands joined in prayer, are interceding for Dante from the height of their blissful thrones.

"Look up now, and do not be afraid," Saint Bernard tells Dante with a smile.

From this moment henceforth Dante feels like one who has just awakened from the most wonderful of dreams and can only recall the warmth and beauty, not the detail, of what he has dreamed. He tries to recapture some of the incandescent light of his dream, but, as each new instant elapses, everything vanishes like snow melting away in a valley flooded with sunshine.

He remembers a ray of light, so vivid, so piercing, so all-encompassing that he would have lost his sight had he turned his eyes away from it—quite the opposite of what would happen to one who tried to stare at the midday sun.

He also remembers that, emboldened to look farther and longer into that ray, he was finally able to join his glance with the infinite essence of God.

There, in the profundity of that essence, he sees (or saw!) how all the pages that unfold upon the universe are bound with love as into one volume. What we see here on earth, that is,—the substance and accidents of all created things—is bound there, in the very essence of God, as the sheets of a book are glued and held together in the spine of the book itself.

Dante's mind, astonished, rapt, immobile in this last and first light, craves no other bliss than that of losing itself in its imperishable delight. No other glow can now please his intellect, for, once perfection has been tasted, all other food is tasteless.

How long can Dante bear that ray of splendor?

This he can only recall—that the deeper his gaze, the more varied that light appears to his glance. But well he knows that it is he, not the light, that is changing.

He sees, in the transparent abyss of that one ray, three circles of three different colors but of one dimension. The first is reflected by the second while the third proceeds equally from the first and the second, like a fire steadily burning. A rainbow plus another plus another—one rainbow that is three rainbows yet three rainbows that are still one.

Dante looks at the three circles with an effort to comprehend how one can contain, and be contained by, the others. Finally, he is struck by something painted on the second of them—his own face, his own human face.

He understands what he sees; but how could such thing ever happen? He understands that the three circles represent the Father, the Son, and the Holy Spirit, respectively, and that, consequently, his own human nature is, at this moment, one with the human nature of Christ, the the Holy Spirit, respectively, and that, consequently, his own human nature is, at this moment, one with the human nature of Christ, the second person of the Trinity. But how did this occur? How could his own human figure ever adapt itself to the form of the circle so perfectly as to seem purposely made for it?

A geometer may sooner solve the insoluble problem of the quadrature of the circle than Dante find out how his own human face could, at that moment, look like Christ's, therefore, like God's.

His wings cannot fly so high, and his mind is suddenly struck by the lightning of a new ray which utterly fulfills all its longing.

The vision of God lasts the infinitesimal fragment of an instant, but in that instant Dante and, with him, all mankind discover the secrets of love—God's love that moves the sun and all the stars.